PETER DYNAMITE
TWICE BORN RUSSIAN

PETER
DYNAMITE

TWICE BORN RUSSIAN:
THE CAPTIVATING STORY OF PETER DEYNEKA SR.

BY NORMAN ROHRER AND PETER DEYNEKA JR.

FOREWORD BY ROBERT W. PROVOST

Anniversary Edition © 2005
Slavic Gospel Association
6151 Commonwealth Drive
Loves Park, Illinois 61111

Printed in the United States of America.

ISBN 1-56773-034-5

This book was originally published by Baker Book House Company, Grand Rapids, Michigan, copyright © 1975, and is reprinted by permission. Scripture quotations in this new edition are from the New King James Version, copyright © 1979, 1980, 1982, 1990 by Thomas Nelson, Inc.

TABLE OF CONTENTS

FOREWORD

This is the story of a 15-year-old Belarussian immigrant whose family borrowed funds to send him to America, hoping he could earn money to send back and help them weather troubled times. But the Lord had much more in store for young Peter Deyneka.

While working hard in his new country, Peter was dramatically converted through the ministry of Dr. Paul Rader at Moody Memorial Church in Chicago. Following his conversion, Peter became consumed by the desire to reach his own people with the Gospel — a task made much more difficult since his homeland was firmly under the iron rule of atheistic communism at the time.

Undaunted as a young man in a foreign land, Peter shared his vision with all who would listen. In 1934, a group of Christian businessmen in Chicago helped him form the Russian Gospel Association, later to become Slavic Gospel Association.

Through the years, there were many challenges as well as many tremendous blessings. Peter established international offices in Australia, Canada, France, New Zealand, and the United Kingdom. Thousands of biblical Russian-language radio programs produced by SGA blanketed the former Soviet Union and helped sustain the believers in their faith. Untold numbers of oppressed people across the lands of Russia could hear the Word of God in no other way. SGA missionaries were spread out across the globe, serving Bible-preaching churches and sharing the Gospel with Russian sailors, immigrants, and visitors at every opportunity.

Claiming God's promise recorded in Jeremiah 33:3 — "Call to Me, and I will answer you, and show you great and mighty things, which you do not know" — Peter frequently traversed the globe, preaching so powerfully that he became known as Peter Dynamite. God used him to raise up a massive and enduring global prayer movement. Two years after he was promoted to glory in 1987, the Lord answered Peter's prayers of a lifetime and the prayers of millions whom he had inspired to pray. Surprising the entire world, the Lord brought the Iron Curtain crashing down. Before our very eyes, He opened the door for the Gospel to 500 million souls who had been held captive by the communist regime.

It is a joyful occasion for SGA to once again make available this inspiring biography of a distinguished servant of Christ. As you read this book, it is important to remember that it was originally written during the oppressive Soviet era when Christians were being severely persecuted. Yet despite how it was, Peter's constant prayer was for freedom to preach the Gospel to all Russians. Nine decades after he boarded that ship for America, he has left a worldwide legacy of prayer and a ministry built solidly upon the principles found in God's Word. Seventeen years after his homegoing, SGA continues to steadfastly pursue his biblical vision — and by God's grace, the mission continues to go forward for the glory of Jesus Christ.

DR. ROBERT W . PROVOST
president of Slavic Gospel Association

PREFACE

You couldn't be with Peter Deyneka very long without God doing something special for your soul. Even casual conversation was a blessing, and listening to Peter preach (in his own inimitable Russian accent and style) filled your heart so full that you would want to shout.

The greatest blessing of all was praying with Peter Deyneka. Peter was one of the first friends to telephone me when I went to pastor Moody Church in Chicago. "I want to come over and pray with you," he said. Many times we were on our knees in my study, crying out to God for His blessing on our lives and ministries. What a prayer warrior Peter was! What answers we saw! I will never forget those all-night prayer meetings that he conducted for us in past Youth for Christ days. "Much prayer — much power!" was more than a motto in those difficult days. It was the secret of God's blessing — and it still is.

This book will get to your heart. None of the facts are exaggerated or embellished, for the life and ministry of Russian-born Peter Deyneka needs no embellishment. For more than 55 years, God gave him a great missionary vision for lost souls — not only for the evangelization of his own Slavic people, but for others as well. Moreover, through the ministry of this dynamic revivalist, thousands of young people around the world gave their lives to Christian service.

As you read this book you will find your faith growing, your desire for prayer increasing, and your concern for lost souls deepening. When this begins to happen, surrender yourself afresh to the Lord and do whatever He tells you to do. God will use you, as He used Peter Deyneka, to touch the lives of others and to help reach a lost world for Jesus Christ.

It was a privilege to know Peter Deyneka. My prayer is that reading this book will do for you what knowing Peter Deyneka did for so many of us. If your heart is open to the Lord, I believe it will.

DR. WARREN W. WIERSBE
author, former senior pastor of Moody Church

INTRODUCTION

Golden rays of a Siberian sunrise were illuminating the gabled peak of their sanctuary as Russian believers streamed inside to worship one morning in 1965. Many who had no Bibles of their own had braved the chill dawn to hear a pastor read from the pulpit Bible. Soon the church was jammed with over 2,000 worshipers united in prayer.

"Oh, God!" cried a young man, his voice trembling. "Save millions of our people here in Russia through the Gospel broadcasts!"

"Yes, Lord, hear his prayer," the congregation responded in unison.

"Encourage our brothers and sisters who are in difficulties," a weeping grandmother prayed.

"Yes, Lord," came again the great, swelling response.

"Bless our brethren in other countries who are evangelizing our nation via the long arms of radio," added an elderly man.

On the high platform that Sunday morning stood a tall, balding visitor. He carried an American passport, but he had the tongue of a native Russian. At the mention of radio ministry, the visiting speaker wept. Fifty years earlier he had left Russia for the New World. There he had found not only a new world but a new life, a personal revolution through the Gospel of Jesus Christ.

In his preaching to millions of people, traveling over two million miles on the King's business, and in his establishment of a missionary-sending agency to the Slavic world, the man had been the first to preach the Gospel by radio to the vast reaches of the Soviet Union. And now, once more among his own people, the visitor discovered that radio broadcasts were a most fruitful means of evangelizing a closed, atheistic land.

Half a century! Yet so great was Peter Deyneka's joy that he wished he could somehow turn back the calendar of passing years and once again walk with his Lord over the same path of tears and triumph.

1

Sure, All Right

The westbound train streaked past the southside tenements, plunged with a roar under the city's bower of concrete, then shuddered to a halt with a hiss of billowing steam.

"Chicago — Union Station!"

A teenager in dark clothing nervously clutched his suitcase and gazed apprehensively at the unfamiliar surroundings. His pockets bulged with a few remaining apples, his only food since disembarking from the Russian ocean liner *S.S. Dvinsk* and boarding the Chicago-bound train in Halifax, Nova Scotia.

"Union Station!" the conductor repeated, opening the doors with a loud clang.

The teenager hesitated for a moment, then stepped down onto the platform of the strange city. That small step would be divinely ordered to lay the groundwork for the evangelization of Slavic people worldwide, although the thought was far from the teenager's mind at that moment.

As the youth walked from the train, a United States customs officer approached. "May I see your papers?" he asked.

The immigrant lad fished in his pockets and withdrew an envelope which he handed to the man in uniform. The papers read: "Peter Deyneka. Born: Staramlynia, province of Grodno, Russia, 1898."

The man studied Peter. "Do you have relatives in Chicago?"

Peter handed him a second note which read, "Cousin Walter Markawitz, Halsted and Maxwell Streets."

The customs officer called a cab and gave the driver instructions. Peter loaded his luggage into the taxi and climbed aboard for the final leg of his long journey.

The Chicago River made him homesick for the Yaseldah River that flowed through Chomsk. Perhaps at that very moment his father was fishing the night waters half a world away. "The fish know Nahum Deyneka and Nahum Deyneka knows the fish," the villagers would say admiringly.

The old cab rattled and whined through the cobblestone streets as the immigrant leaned back and reflected on his voyage from Chomsk in the Old World.

On March 3, 1914, many Deyneka relatives and their close friends crowded into the little house to wish the traveler good fortune. The singing, interspersed with small glasses of vodka, drove away the sadness in true Russian fashion.

"Hey, Pyotr!" his brother Andrei exclaimed, interrupting the party. "Look at this — from Misha!"

"A whole bottle of vodka? Misha must be drunk."

"Misha says you should drink to him for good luck and for plenty of money in America," the younger brother commanded. "First, though, show everyone here how you speak English."

The older brother was embarrassed and protested strongly. "But Andrei, I don't know much English."

"Don't be bashful," Andrei shouted. "You speak it well — just like a real American. I heard you."

Andrei had stepped up onto a chair and clapped his hands. "Listen, everyone! My brother Pyotr is going to show how they talk in America."

The murmur of Slavic voices grew still as the guest of honor shrugged. "My brother is making a joke," Peter said meekly. "He knows I don't know much English . . ."

The crowd shouted and clapped. "Speech!"

"He's just bashful," Andrei insisted, "Go ahead, Pyotr. Say something in English."

With a red face, the young man bound for the land of opportunity mounted the chair and cleared his throat. "Sure, all right," he said quietly in English.

The villagers shouted and applauded. "You see?" Andrei exclaimed, "Just like a real American. Do it again, Pyotr."

"Sure, all right."

The crowd tried to repeat it. "Shoor-r. All-r-rayt." What an outlandish language English seemed to be!

After a good time of fellowship, Peter's father brought around the rented horse and wagon that would take his son to the train station.

"Please be careful, son," his mother pleaded.

"Yes, Mama," Peter replied, carrying his bags to the wagon.

"Do not trust strangers."

"No, mama."

"Save your money and send as much home as you can. We have borrowed many rubles to send you to America. The interest on the money is high. We will need all you can send to pay it off."

"I know," Peter said as he kissed her one last time.

Villagers waved their good wishes as Peter and his father rolled through the dirt streets in the horse-drawn wagon carrying a few suitcases and the huge bag of garlic and salami sandwiches. The farther they traveled on the 25-mile journey to the train station, the more Peter's father regretted his decision to send his eldest son to America. It now seemed like a bad dream.

As the train approached, the father clung to his son. "Pyotr," he sobbed, "this train will take you away from me and I may never see you again." But the one-way ticket had been purchased — there was no opportunity to turn back now.

On March 11, 1914, Peter sailed from Libau, Russia, bound for Halifax, Nova Scotia. For 14 days and nights, the sturdy Russian ship tossed and churned through the stormy Atlantic. Peter had never sailed before. Consequently, his mother prepared a lunch for him, packed to last the whole voyage. It was so large that an older friend carried it on board ship for him.

Peter regularly went to the deck for exercise and daily ate his black bread and garlic — a diet he credited with preventing the terrible seasickness that gripped so many of the other passengers.

During the first days at sea, Peter had met some of the Russian sailors on the ship. The sailors conspired to trick the naive boy from the country.

"If you help us work in the kitchen, we will give you meals in return," the wily sailors promised Peter.

Dutifully, Peter worked for his meals all across the Atlantic. Every day he longingly looked through the window of the door leading into the ship's dining room and envied all of the wealthy people who were able to eat in the luxurious surroundings. It wasn't until the last day of the voyage Peter learned that the purchase of a boat ticket also included three meals a day in the ship's dining room.

But Peter's misfortune was later to provide an excellent sermon illustration which he often used in his later evangelistic ministry. "I was like many people who are trying to work for their salvation and do not know that our Heavenly Father has already provided it for free through Jesus Christ," Peter would say.

━━┼═◇═┼━━

"Halsted and Maxwell," the Chicago taxi driver announced, motioning toward a small house as he brought his car to a stop.

"Poydítye vi," Peter spoke excitedly in Russian to the driver.

The cabbie understood and went to the door, "There's a young man here from the Old Country," he announced to the boarder who appeared at the door.

"Is anyone expecting you?" the man asked.

"Sure, all right," Peter replied.

When Walter Markawitz returned from work at six, he was surprised to find young Peter there. "This house is already full of boarders," Walter sighed, "but I guess you can stay."

Peter cried himself to sleep that night in the strange city. If only his elder brother Stephan had lived. He was the one who had been chosen to seek the family's fortune in America.

What if I fail! Peter thought. *What if Mama and Papa, Vasily, Maksim, Andrei, Ivan, Anastacia, and Tekla lose the house and the land they mortgaged to send me to America!*

One hundred dollars — that was the equivalent of two hundred rubles at that time. If he could earn that much, the Deynekas could pay all their debts and be relatively wealthy.

Peter listened in the darkness to the hum of the city. The new country was alive with industry and progress. The Markawitzes' house was warm. Perhaps he would not have to take his turn sleeping on top of a brick oven as he often had done in Russia when winter came.

The lonely boy could scarcely imagine that the unseen hand of Providence had brought him halfway around the globe like a chess maneuver in a strategy for evangelical outreach that would one day bless millions of Russian people. This frightened young immigrant with no money, no job, and no living faith seemed at that moment an unlikely candidate for such a historic career.

Peter's first sunrise in the new world found him on the street, joining the unemployed who were seeking work. Gradually the refrain became familiar: "That's all we're hiring. No more today!"

Peter would bow and reply, "Sure, all right," and go home disappointed. But he would try again, for he had adopted the motto of his new city: "I will!"

Chicago was rapidly becoming America's second-largest metropolis. In this growing city, it was appropriate that young Peter should find his first job in a lumberyard supplying building material. He earned $6.90 a week. No assignment was too hard for his eager hands, except when he didn't understand the orders.

One day the foreman gave Peter hurried instructions. "Sure, all right," Peter replied, afraid to admit that he had understood nothing. When the foreman returned to find the job undone, he threatened to fire the Russian. "Sure, all right," Peter replied, looking around for a "fire." But he wasn't fired, and left the following year for a better job at the Crane Company machine shop. Crane paid its employees in refined gold, handing out little envelopes containing the precious ore as paychecks.

Russian immigrants in Chicago who were activists with the International Workers of the World began calling on Peter. Twice a week they would visit him at the boarding house, urging him to join their ranks. "We're going to change the world!" they boasted. "There is no God. We're going to make the world better ourselves!"

Peter hesitated. His ties to the Russian Orthodox Church were strong. "There are two gods." his mother had told him. "One is in heaven; the other is the czar of Russia." But the constant outpouring of propaganda by the Chicago atheists finally convinced him they were right.

Half a world away, the Deyneka family lived in daily suspense. If Pyotr failed in the New World, all their hopes of freedom from servitude to their lenders would be gone. He told them nothing of his new allegiance to atheism, nor that he attended meetings of the IWW. He sent his family as much money as he could squeeze from his small paycheck. He lived on dried bread and salami, spending an occasional dollar on theaters, dancing, smoking, or drinking. Yet there was an emptiness in his heart as he searched in vain for lasting peace. However, his hard work and good stewardship paid off the family debt in one year.

✦—+—☰◈☲—+—✦

On a Sunday afternoon stroll, Peter was surprised to hear the strains of a hymn in his native tongue coming from five Russian men at Union and 13th streets. He listened cautiously from a safe position across the street. That afternoon in 1916, as a lad of 18 years, he heard for the first time the revolutionary message that Christ died for sinners, and that by faith in Him a believer could have peace with God. The meeting finally broke up and Peter went home.

The following Sunday he was back, this time gathering courage to cross the street and talk to the Russians. "If you receive the Lord Jesus Christ, He will save you from sin," the strangers promised. "You would not need to drink or go to dance halls to find joy."

Peter shook his head. Surely these were the only five men in the world who believed such a message.

The weeks passed. Peter moved to a home where he lived with several Russian-Americans. He studied newspapers to learn English and to enjoy the pictures.

"Look here," he exclaimed one evening as he settled down to read. "A baseball player is preaching on the east side."

"That's Billy Sunday," his roommate replied as he dressed to go out.

"I want to hear him," Peter announced.

"If you go, don't take any money."

"Why not?"

"They might rob you."

Peter looked at the article again. He decided to see the ball player, regardless of the "danger." But in case his roommate was right, he took just one dollar.

He found the hall packed with people. They made the walls ring with their singing. Homer Rodeheaver played an instrument which Peter later learned was a trombone. Everything was so different. In Russia, the Orthodox priest was a symbol of fear. But in America, Peter noticed that the people seemed to be happy in church.

Billy Sunday paced the platform as he began to preach. Peter winced when the preacher smashed a chair to dramatically illustrate a point in his lightning-fast delivery. Peter gripped the dollar bill in his right pocket and wondered if this was when the "robbery" would take place.

Peter didn't understand the invitation to receive Christ. When he spotted an altar counselor looking at him, he gripped his dollar more tightly. When the man walked up and extended his hand, Peter held on to his money and extended his left hand. As soon as he could, he escaped into the streets, vowing he would never go to such a place again.

"What did Billy Sunday have to say?" his roommate asked.

"He talked about Jesus Christ."

"Is that all?"

"That's all I could understand," Peter admitted.

A Russian couple, with intentions like Priscilla and Aquila of the New Testament, invited young Peter to live in their house. They saw the move as an evangelistic opportunity. Peter viewed it as a chance to eat home-made borscht and speak Russian again.

"Don't worry," he promised his buddies. "I'll never believe that Christian stuff."

Often when believers came to the home, Peter would flee to his room and shut the door. He heard that the entire local evangelical Russian church was praying for him, but he resolutely held fast to his pretended atheism. He remained in that home for only a few months, finally moving in exasperation to an American home.

Peter remembered that the Christians he had heard on the street corner told him he could hear eloquent English spoken at a place called Moody Memorial Church on Clark Street and North Avenue. He decided to attend, and expected to find a small auditorium with a handful of old people. Instead, he found 4,000 people of all ages sitting on wooden benches in a huge tabernacle with sawdust sprinkled on the floor.

"More Christians?" Peter murmured. He was tempted to leave, but the beauty of the music held him. Besides, it was Sunday and there was nothing better to do.

As Paul Rader preached his sermon, Peter felt smaller and smaller. He was convinced that someone had tipped off the preacher about the young Russian's sinful life. "You there, you need to be born again!" Rader shouted time after time, pointing his long finger at the audience, always seeming to pick Peter out of the crowd. Peter's heart raced. How could this man know so much about him — a total stranger?

Peter detected another voice that evening, a conviction inside him, speaking unmistakably: *You are a lost sinner . . . Christ died for you . . . whoever believes in Him will not perish.*

But the altar counselors frightened him, so Peter left. Yet he did plan to return on another Sunday for the "free English lessons" and the inspiring music. He even obtained a *Jesus Saves* button for his lapel so the counselors wouldn't bother him and try to take him to the prayer room. He was suspicious about what went on behind those closed doors in that room up front.

One Sunday, Peter attended the young men's Bible class taught by Harry Herring at 3:00 on Sunday afternoons. Seventy-five young men attended this lively Bible class. At the close of his teaching, Mr. Herring asked, "Would you raise your hand if you would like to be remembered in prayer today?" Peter raised his hand.

That Sunday night, Peter wore his *Jesus Saves* lapel button to the evening service. After a great evangelistic message, Paul Rader invited those who wanted to accept the Lord as their personal Savior to come to the altar. During the invitation, Peter whispered to a friend who sat near him, "You ought to go forward and get saved."

"I'll go if you'll go with me," came the reply.

"Okay. Let's go."

Peter outwalked his friend and bravely went first into the prayer room where Christian workers with their Bibles were ready to help those seeking salvation. Peter knelt and wept before God, realizing he was a lost sinner without Christ.

That night, Peter left his old life behind. His days forever after would be different. The date was January 18, 1920. Peter was 21.

His landlord noticed Peter's broad smile when he returned home that night, "What's wrong with you, Peter? Are you drunk?" he asked.

"No, I'm not drunk. I'm saved."

"Go to bed. You'll feel all right in the morning," the man assured. But Peter couldn't sleep all night, lying wide awake with joy.

The smile arose with him the next day. "Peter," his landlord objected, "You're still drunk."

"No," Peter insisted, "I'm a new person."

God had "sought for a man among them who would make a wall, and stand in the gap before [Him] on behalf of the land" (Ezekiel 22:30). And He had found him.

2

VISIONS OF A DYING WORLD

Centuries ago a Russian Orthodox monk named Philotheus exclaimed in a burst of patriotism and piety, "Light and truth have found their eternal home in Moscow!"

Peter Deyneka had found the Light and Truth, but not in Russia. He had come to America restive and withdrawn, but now it seemed he could not talk to enough people to share the joy of his spiritual birth. He found himself testifying for the Lord at work, on street corners, in Gospel missions, and to individuals wherever he met them. Each conversation fired his zeal even hotter, causing him to grow in his determination to become a soul-winner.

He joined Moody Memorial Church and attended all the meetings. He was present at Bible conferences, became elected president of the large young men's Bible class, joined the Ushers' Band to expand opportunities to speak to people about Jesus Christ, and somehow found time to enroll for evening classes at Moody Bible Institute.

Peter seldom attended church without soldiers, sailors, policemen, or children in tow. In testimony meetings, he was always the first one on his feet. Pastor Paul Rader noticed the young firebrand who became fondly known to the congregation as Peter Dynamite, a play on his last name and his explosive speaking style.

On July 25, 1921, Peter was baptized at Cedar Lake, Indiana, where Moody Church sponsored Bible conferences. While working at the camp, Peter looked for young men to talk to about Christ. One Sunday afternoon near the railroad station, where many vacationers were waiting for the train, he gave his testimony at a street meeting. Peter noticed two young men sitting nearby on a bench, dressed for an evening out. Peter approached them and asked, "Do you mind if I sit by you?"

They studied him for a moment, then moved over to give him room. "We're going to the dance," they said.

"You should come to the Gospel meeting tonight."

"No, we have dates with two girls at the dance hall," they replied.

"Well, I'm going to pray that the Lord will save your souls tonight. You come to the conference grounds at any time and ask for me."

The young men laughed and quickly left.

Back at the conference grounds, Peter found a Christian brother and asked him to pray for the two men headed for the dance. Two hours later, the same two men came to the Bible conference grounds and asked for Peter Deyneka.

"Do you remember us?" they asked.

Peter nodded. "Glad to see you again."

"We came to tell you that we want to accept the Lord Jesus Christ as our Savior. Will you pray for us?"

Peter quickly took them to the prayer room behind the tabernacle where they were wonderfully converted.

"Why did you leave the dance?" Peter asked.

They explained that after he had talked to them at the station, they felt uncomfortable. While they were dancing, some misunderstanding arose between them and their girlfriends. Disgruntled, they left their dates to find Peter. Those men were two of many people the young Russian led to Christ during his frequent trips to Cedar Lake.

Each Sunday afternoon, Peter's Bible class met at Moody Church from 3:00 to 4:00 p.m. After the class, Peter would cross North Avenue and hand out tracts in Lincoln Park as he spoke to strangers about the Lord. The park was usually sprinkled with sailors in training at the nearby Great Lakes Naval Training Station on the northern edge of Chicago.

One day Peter noticed two sailors on a bench in the park. He also spotted three sailors on another bench. First he approached the two and asked, "Are you looking for real joy?"

"Of course!" they replied sheepishly.

"Well," Peter explained, "let me tell you how you can find the greatest joy in the world."

For several minutes, he boldly shared his testimony with them. "If you would like to know more about how to get this joy, come and hear a great preacher at Moody Memorial Church tonight," he said, pointing to the nearby wooden tabernacle that was then Moody Church. "Meet me at 6:30 and we'll have something to eat first."

The agreement was made, so Peter made his way to the three sailors on another bench to repeat the invitation.

At 6:30 he bought hot dogs for five sailors and then took them to the service, seating them in the front row. A brass band played vigorous music for half an hour while the people gathered. A choir of 200 sat behind the speaker. The music set the spirit for the message by Paul Rader.

At the invitation, all five sailors looked at Peter for encouragement, wondering what to do. Peter nodded. "Sure, go ahead, raise your hands," he whispered. All five obeyed.

The congregation began singing *Just As I Am*, and people moved toward the counseling rooms. Again, the sailors looked at Peter. He nodded, encouraging them to go forward. One of them whispered, "If you don't mind, we'd like you to come with us."

"Sure, I'll be happy to," Peter said, getting up and starting for a prayer room with his five charges in tow. Since he had told them all he knew in his broken English, he waited outside while the counselors spoke to the men about their eternal salvation.

When the men came out of the room, Peter knew that each had taken the step of faith. Their faces shone. They hugged Peter and thanked him for introducing them to Jesus Christ.

The five sailors scattered to the four winds, but for a long time they kept in touch with Peter through correspondence.

＋—＋　 ⊨◊⊨　—＋—　＋

In the early days of his Christian life, Peter attended all the missionary conferences at Moody Memorial Church. In one service, Peter was unusually attentive because Pastor Rader continually made reference to the need for workers in the "corn" field. Was it actually so? Did the Lord need workers in the "corn" field?

Peter listened closely. He was hoping to hear of a need for workers among his own Slavic people, but the speaker did not mention Russia. He kept calling for workers in the "corn" field instead.

At the close of the meeting Peter responded to the invitation. His heart was so moved that he wanted to eagerly serve the Lord wherever the need was greatest, even if it meant the "corn" field. Only after the service had ended did he discover that Pastor Rader was appealing for workers in the "foreign" field!

Many Christians since have clearly understood the need for workers in foreign fields and have done nothing. Peter misunderstood the call and was uncertain of the conditions, but he obeyed first and learned the conditions later.

A faithful member of Moody Church named Andrew Wyzenbeek operated a thriving machine shop in Chicago. This Christian businessman's policy was to hire a certain number of young men who might be inexperienced but who needed a job as they prepared themselves for Christian service. Mr. Wyzenbeek held daily prayer meetings and Bible studies for employees in his machine shop, and encouraged his young men to actively pursue their commitment to the Lord's work.

Peter Deyneka became one of Mr. Wyzenbeek's protégés. Every day the employer spoke to Peter about pursuing his Christian training. This bighearted, generous man paid Peter well and was a valued friend in setting him on the path of full commitment.

After working for several seasons in Wyzenbeek's machine shop, Peter felt ready to take a step toward Christian training. He sought advice from Pastor Rader. As they discussed his plans in the church office, Mr. Rader reached for the telephone and called J. D. Williams, president of St. Paul Bible School in Minnesota, hoping to enroll Peter in the school's 1922 fall term. Right there on the phone, the enrollment was completed. Peter was on his way to school.

That summer Peter worked at Cedar Lake Christian Conference Center with his boss, Andrew Wyzenbeek. Young friends at Moody Church obeyed their pastor's advice to "fill Peter's pockets with money" at a surprise sendoff party, providing the means of travel to Bible school.

In St. Paul, Peter enjoyed a series of life-changing experiences. President and Mrs. J. D. Williams took seriously their responsibilities in guiding the school. They spent many hours in prayer for the student body and the progress of the institution. Many times they would take a hotel room in St. Paul and spend the entire day in prayer concerning the needs of the school and its students. Thus all the activities were bathed in intercession. The new student noted this and never forgot these important lessons on the power of prayer.

The school was located in a renovated old mansion in the midway area between St. Paul and Minneapolis. Peter's first professor, Harold Freleigh, was impressed by his new student's zeal and helped him through discouraging times. The Russian lad was frequently ready to quit the academic life because he couldn't master English grammar. Mr. Freleigh would call together a few students who were Peter's special friends and who knew how to talk to the Lord. Together, they would pull him through.

School policy directed that each Friday afternoon students would engage in personal evangelism, distributing tracts and talking to people. Saturday nights found them at a downtown mission, leading the meeting. These assignments greatly appealed to Peter. During his first year, he personally led 65 people to Christ. One of these was a Frenchman whom Peter met on University Avenue in St. Paul. The man had approached Peter with a piece of paper asking in a heavy accent, "Can you show me the way to this address?"

"No," Peter admitted, "but I can show you the way to heaven."

The Frenchman looked at him curiously. "The way to heaven?"

Peter nodded.

"Well, before you tell me the way to heaven, I would like to find my way to this factory," the Frenchman insisted.

Peter quoted John 14:6 and talked to him for approximately 20 minutes. Finally, the Frenchman put the note away in his pocket. "Yes, please show me, for I want to know the way to heaven," he pleaded. A Russian and a Frenchman, standing on a street corner in America, talking about the heavenly kingdom.

Peter took the man to Alliance Tabernacle a few blocks away. The door was locked, so they climbed in through a window — Peter first, the Frenchman following. Inside, they knelt and prayed for salvation as the Frenchman poured out his heart to Christ and asked for the free gift of salvation. He later returned to France as a Christian missionary.

Peter's zeal was boundless. He started a men's all-night prayer meeting at the school, to which an impressive list of missionaries and Christian leaders trace their spiritual maturing. Many times small brush-fire revivals would spring up in those prayer meetings as students were reconciled to each other and became more earnest in their zeal for God. These Friday night prayer meetings continued for many years after Peter graduated.

Following his first year in St. Paul, Peter returned to Chicago and became a night watchman at Chicago Gospel Tabernacle where Paul Rader was now involved in an evangelistic outreach. They had meetings every night, but the sides of the building were open and its two grand pianos on the platform had to be guarded. At night, policemen would often come into the tabernacle to relax or to warm themselves. Peter led many of them to Christ.

During the summer of his third year at school, Peter was assigned by the president of St. Paul Bible School to help start a new church among European immigrants in Aberdeen, South Dakota. At that time, the United States government was giving these immigrants free land if they would homestead in North and South Dakota. They started coming in droves in the early part of 1900, and many thousands of Russians eventually came to these states to farm. In fact, there were large Russian settlements there.

One of these settlements was called Kiev, near the neighboring town of Butte, some 500 miles west of Minneapolis. Peter's first series of meetings was at a little schoolhouse about 11 miles south of Butte. For one full week he preached, and the place was packed with Russian immigrants as well as English-speaking people who lived in the area.

In South Dakota, Peter's host was a farmer who gave him a horse to ride so he could visit surrounding farms and promote his meetings being held at the schoolhouse. But Peter complained to the farmer that he was unable to travel very far because the horse was too slow. So the next day, the farmer offered to give Peter a faster horse "if you aren't afraid to ride him." The preacher assured his host that he was not, and mounted the younger, faster animal.

"Never let go of the reins," the farmer called as he watched the horse bolt for the open road.

Once beyond the farmyard, the horse went so fast Peter could hardly catch his breath. The horse kept going faster and faster, despite repeated demands to stop. Cattle and chickens scattered as the animal thundered down the road. *Lord, stop this horse!* Peter prayed.

Peter finally succeeded in steering the steed toward a farm, but it reared up on its hind legs and would not stop completely. The farmers ran out to see what was happening, just in time to hear Peter shout, "Come and hear the Russian evangelist tonight at the schoolhouse!"

"I visited many farms in just a few hours that day and earned the well-deserved reputation of a Russian Cossack," Peter later recalled.

It rained almost continually during those meetings. Peter had to travel approximately four miles one way from the house where he was staying. He did this every day for a week and eventually became so sore that he could hardly walk into the meeting after he climbed off his horse.

After the week of meetings in the schoolhouse, Peter went into Butte where he found a large Russian settlement. He obtained permission to use the facilities of an English-speaking church and tried to round up all the Russian people. They were suspicious of him, even afraid, but the people eventually got to know and trust the visitor. The offering for the week was $5, and Peter was quite happy. He found himself spending the entire summer in this type of pioneer ministry.

In Butte, Peter began eating Russian food again which he hadn't had at the Bible school. One woman would make borscht and Peter relished all he could get. He wanted nothing more. "You can eat everything else," he told the people of other nationalities who sometimes gathered at the table. "I'll take the borscht."

When he returned to St. Paul, the young Russian felt the burden for evangelizing his own people increasing. Mr. and Mrs. Steven Tovstenko, who had been working with him in the Minneapolis area, urged him to remain in America. "Why don't you stay here?" they reasoned. "We need you to work in the United States."

"No, I must go back to Russia because the many unsaved there must hear the Gospel," Peter insisted. "I must also reach my own family with the Gospel."

The summer before his final year of school, Peter made another trip to South Dakota — this time to Webster — with a couple other St. Paul students. Not knowing one person in town, the team rented a hall on Main Street for three weeks and paid one week's rent in advance. They also rented chairs, installed electric lights, and placed signs outside the hall to announce the meetings.

Only a few curious children came the first night to hear the singing. But when the preaching began, they ran outside. After the meeting, the three evangelists — Fred Shelander, Howard Kellec, and Peter — set up sleeping accommodations on the floor in back of the hall, having no money left for food or lodging. They prayed until about 3:00 a.m., then spread their newspapers out and tried to sleep.

"Let's get out of here," one of the men finally suggested, getting to his feet. "I can't imagine it's the Lord's will for us to be sleeping on this cold, hard floor."

Peter urged him to be patient, to trust the Lord and "go through." He was convinced they were being tested for a reason. "Testings and trials are good for a person," he reminded them. "They refine the soul and produce a vessel unto honor that God can use."

After that night, a lady who had come to one of the services asked the three young men where they were staying. They told her they were sleeping on newspapers on the floor in back of the auditorium. She seemed surprised and quickly arranged for the men to stay in homes of Christians in the area.

On another night, Howard began to sing right in the middle of his sermon. Peter asked him afterward what kind of preaching it was where you started singing in the middle of talking. But this technique became a popular addition to Peter's own preaching later on, adding great blessing in the midst of sermons, all-night prayer meetings, and revival meetings.

During the third night of the series, the men conducted a street meeting in front of the hall before the evening service. Howard Kellec was giving his testimony, quoting the passage of Scripture where Jesus said He would gather us under His wings as a hen does her chicks, but the people were not responding and — once again — would not accept the invitation. As Howard thought of the lost souls in Webster, he began to weep.

That night was a turning point as the South Dakotans took note and were affected by Howard's genuine concern. As a result, many new people began coming to the services. The campaign continued, and children's meetings were added in the afternoon. Eventually, because of those meetings, a congregation was organized in Webster.

The experiences on the Dakota plains seemed to toughen Peter's resolve to continue preaching. During his final year of school he took a full load of classes, traveled by train each Friday afternoon to Mason City, Iowa, visited all day on Saturday, preached on Sunday, and caught an all-night train back to St. Paul to arrive home in time for classes on Monday morning. He kept up this grueling schedule for the entire school year until graduation in 1925.

For the commencement ceremony of his class, Peter was chosen to give the address. His English was the poorest in the school, but his heart burned the hottest for the eternal things that mattered most. The energetic

Russian won lasting friendships among the students at St. Paul. In his yearbook they wrote their endearments . . .

> Remember as you journey along the straight and narrow way that you have a friend who will *never, ever* forget you. God has many people in this old world, but only one like you, Peter. I love you because God made you just like you are.
> — Ernie Brown; Omaha, Nebraska

> I thank God for the day I met you and for leading me to accept Christ as my Savior. I will always remember the good times we have had in Room 14. Thank you for all your advice and your prayers.
> — Roy Petersen; Dawson, Minnesota

> I love you because the love of Christ dwells in you. I shall never forget the blessed times we had together in prayer and in fellowship during these days at Bible school. Though we will soon be separated one from another, we still will meet at the blood-bought mercy seat. I trust the Lord will keep you humble at the feet of Jesus and continue to use you to pluck the brands from the burning . . .
> — Oliver K. Cedar; Bethel, Minnesota

> Always be yourself . . . with Christ added.
> — Leona Kjorth; St. Paul, Minnesota

> Your ringing testimonies for our loving Lord I shall never forget. They have meant much to me. I praise God that you have greatly influenced my life. I am so thankful that I ever knew Peter the Russian, a child of the King.
> — Cora Belle Nuing; St. Paul, Minnesota

The Lord sustained Peter Deyneka physically, spiritually, and mentally during his years at St. Paul Bible College. Down on his knees scrubbing dormitory floors in those cold Minnesota winters, Peter learned obedience. As he scrubbed, he prayed. And at the end of it all, he was able to finish school with all his bills paid.

3

FIVE MILLION CORPSES

From 1918 to 1922, Peter Deyneka received no letters from his family in Russia. During that period, a famine of enormous proportions had settled on Russia, eroding the foundations of society and briefly halting the onrush of the Bolsheviks to construct their new brand of government.

The end of the long civil war had promised to usher in a new social order. However, the devastated country could not struggle to its feet to accept the challenges. Indescribable human suffering descended upon Russia. Their society was in disarray. The only thing uniting the country at that time was a common misery in the aftermath of the terrible war. They had survived the war, but could they survive the hazards of peace?

At the heart of the problem was the peasant. Although the common people had theoretically gained control of the land which had formerly belonged to the rich or to the State, they hated the new regime's collectivism and would not agree to the prescribed ratio of earnings from their own crops. The peasants clashed with the government over these new economic policies and responded by harvesting only enough food for their own minimum subsistence. This led to a severe decline in food production that gradually threatened the cities with starvation. Transportation facilities also came to a standstill.

On top of this tremendous social turmoil came unparalleled drought in the early 1920s. Lack of rain paralyzed agriculture just as war had paralyzed industry. The immense impact of the twin disasters was a tragedy that shocked the world.

A large section of southeastern Russia, notably the farmland around the lower Volga River, yielded practically no crops whatsoever. About 50 million people faced death by starvation. An estimated five million people died from malnutrition.

At this time, the Russian writer Maxim Gorky made an appeal to the American people through Herbert Hoover. However, many Soviets were wary of Hoover's assistance, fearing he would use it as a political weapon. On August 20, 1921, an agreement was finally reached between the American Relief Administration (ARA) and the Soviet government. By the end of September, shipments of food began to arrive in Russia.

The aid continued for two years, but the noble efforts of the ARA and the Red Cross could reach only a fifth of the suffering people. In July 1923, grateful Russians thanked the U.S. organization and Herbert Hoover. A missive to the ARA stated that the Russian people promised "never to forget the help given by the American people through the ARA, seeing in it a pledge of the future of the two nations."

During this unprecedented calamity, the church increased its ministry to a tragically needy people. "I cannot describe what joy we felt as we received food parcels," the great Russian preacher Ivan S. Prokhanov declared. "Without exaggeration, I can say that the ARA saved millions of lives from starvation. The Russian people who survived those days will never forget that brotherly help from the American people."

Hundreds of thousands of people were not as fortunate. They did not have stamina or faith enough to overcome the horror of those days. Each day the newspapers were filled with reports of suicides. Typhus and cholera epidemics took thousands of other lives.

Into the void of agony and political disarray came great opportunities for Christian witnessing. Believers tried to instill hope, offering prayer and reading Scripture. The Evangelical Christian Union under Prokhanov's leadership obtained funds in America to print and distribute 60,000 Bibles and New Testaments. Such religious liberties were brief, and after that time importing Bibles from abroad was forbidden.

The world was watching closely in those days to see which political path Russia would follow. Would communism continue? Or would the floundering new society change course?

Peter Deyneka's family had caught the full impact of the dreadful starvation plague. Three brothers and two sisters perished from hunger before Peter learned of the tragedy. The notice arrived while he was working as a night watchman at Chicago Gospel Tabernacle. It was the first letter he had received from his family in five years, and the news devastated him. He could hardly eat or sleep, and spent entire nights in prayer for his family.

Peter's own relatives had never heard the Gospel of God's grace — that which had revolutionized his life. His heart burned to tell his people of the hope of salvation and eternal life. Peter sent home what money he could, knowing it wouldn't be enough, and prayed for an opportunity to become a missionary to his people.

During this period of tragedy, he came upon a report from Oswald J. Smith who had toured Russia and its border countries on a preaching mission. The report told of spiritual awakenings in Eastern Europe and called for prayer on behalf of the people.

"How can I describe my experiences?" Smith wrote. "How can I tell what my eyes have seen and my ears have heard? Words fail me as I seek to unburden my heart and convey to others the impression of my visit to the mission fields of ancient Russia. Never again can life be the same, nor my ministry continue as it was."

The report told of thronging multitudes, crowded aisles, congested pews, plaintive songs, and fervent prayers from broken people who had known extraordinary suffering.

"Would to God I could do something to alleviate thy sufferings and point thee to the Light!" Smith wrote. "How great thy burden! How long thy night of darkness, pain, and woe!"

Peter determined in his heart that he would trust God to send him to his people with the message of the Gospel. When the war was over, he cabled more money to his parents so they could buy food and hold on to life. This postwar cable provided the first bread his family had seen in five years. He wrote earnestly to his family, sending tracts and long letters, quoting passages of Scripture, and urging them to accept the Lord. Many were the days when his weakened father asked to be propped up near the window so he could watch the road, hoping to see his eldest son approach.

As Peter was seeking the Lord concerning the overwhelming needs in Europe, a series of evangelistic meetings in Minneapolis was offered and he took them. On August 9, 1925, while he was staying in a private home,

Peter distinctly heard the call to return to Russia. He promised God he would go as soon as funds were supplied.

One morning at 6:00 a.m., a knock on the door awakened him. He opened the door to find a lady who had attended one of his meetings. "Peter," she began, with great concern upon her face, "the Lord has spoken to me about selling my diamond ring and giving you $100 toward your trip to Russia." She was the first of many, as other people at his meetings were also prompted to supply funds designated for the trip.

By October 1, 1925, Peter was on board a ship bound for his homeland. He conducted regular services on the ship, keeping on his feet as they passed through churning waters by holding on to a railing while the ship rocked back and forth.

From Bremen, where the ship docked, Peter took the train to Warsaw, Poland, taking along a trunk packed with clothing and several hundred Russian Bibles and New Testaments. From Warsaw, he continued by train to White Russia (Belarus) and his home town of Chomsk. He hired a horse and wagon to travel the last 25 miles from the depot because there was no other means of transportation. The driver was afraid Peter's American clothing would invite a robber, so he threw an old sheepskin over him. "This will make you look more like us," he explained.

They made their way safely through the woods to the little town of Chomsk, two miles from the small village where Peter grew up and which he had left 11 years earlier. But Peter didn't know what he would find at home. He didn't even know if his ailing father would still be alive.

4

UPSIDE DOWN
FOR GOD

Shattered buildings and trees stripped of foliage for food stood as mute evidence that war and famine had stalked the land of Peter's birth during his time in America. As part of the war settlement, the Russian border had been moved, giving Poland a strip of land that included Peter's hometown. (After World War II, Chomsk was reclaimed by Russia.)

Peter arrived in Chomsk on the day of the annual market which brought hundreds of visitors — Russians, Jews, and Poles from many parts of White Russia — to the city of 3,000 people. People from Peter's village just outside Chomsk recognized him immediately as the wagon pulled up. "Wait here!" they cried excitedly. "We will get your mother and brother."

Peter sat on top of his trunk in the wagon and waited, fearing his treasure might be stolen if he left it. Word spread quickly that an "American" had come. Crowds of people in the market pressed closely to the wagon to see the visitor and his fancy clothes and sturdy trunk.

On his high perch, Peter spotted his mother rushing through the crowd with a cluster of villagers in tow. She was crying. The tall son leaped from the wagon and took her in his arms.

"Pyotr!" she could only sob. "Oh, Pyotr . . ."

"Mama," he said tenderly. "It's so good to see you."

"Pyotr, why didn't you come sooner? Papa died just five weeks ago. He wanted to see you. He didn't want to die without seeing you. But now he's gone. If only . . ."

Through her tears, Anastacia Deyneka cursed the dreadful famine that had slain her entire family except Peter and his younger brother Andrei, who stood silently at their side. Peter embraced him.

Eleven years had changed them all — especially Peter. He had written from America that he had become "a new creature in Christ Jesus." Word had spread throughout the villages that a new religion in America had "turned Peter upside down."

Peter ordered the wagon driver to carry them home. He wanted some privacy, but crowds of neighbors followed the wagon. Some asked for vodka to celebrate, others asked for American money, and still others wanted to know about his new faith.

Inside the Deynekas' small, humble, thatched-roof house, the three still found no peace. Villagers swarmed into the home, eager to hear Peter describe his journey to the New World. If they locked the door, people would bang on it and shake the latch until they were forced to open it and let them in.

"Tell me how Papa died," Peter said, noticing the bed that had been arranged beside the front window.

"It was the terrible famine that followed the soldiers," Mrs. Deyneka explained. "We only had grass and weeds to eat. Sometimes we ground acorns. We even tried to make flour from plants and rough leaves, but they cut Papa's mouth and made it bleed. It was terrible." Tears tumbled down her thin cheeks.

By now the house was filled with people demanding to hear Peter speak. Outside people were standing at the windows, anxious to hear his tales about the faraway land. But they were disappointed.

"I have come to tell you about Jesus Christ," Peter announced. "It's true, I have become a new person. Old things have passed away; all things are new."

"We don't understand." his mother objected, "How are you a new creature? You look like my son Pyotr."

Peter began to preach — the first person ever to preach the Gospel of Jesus Christ in his village. People listened eagerly, especially the younger ones who could read and write and were also interested in his Bible.

"The first thing I am going to do is to pray and thank God for the safe journey from America to my Russian home," Peter announced.

"Look!" someone whispered as Peter prayed, "He closed his eyes! How strange! I wonder why."

Others exclaimed, "I've never heard such a prayer before!"

When he had finished someone asked, "Will you please teach me that prayer too?"

Peter later announced to the disappointed villagers that as a Christian he no longer drank, so there would be no vodka to celebrate his homecoming. But the people stayed anyhow, hungrily taking in every word he had to say. He began speaking at approximately 7:00 in the evening. When he finished, it was nearly midnight. Still, the people did not want to go away. He preached the Gospel as simply as he knew how, weaving into his message information about American life and customs. Finally Andrei, who was an atheist, angrily ordered the people to leave so the family could be alone.

"Out! Out!" he demanded, "We have not had one minute alone with my brother and he just this day arrived home. Out!"

The Deynekas talked until 3:00 a.m. Exhausted, Peter lay down on a hard bench and fell asleep. But at sunrise, the neighbors were pounding on the door and shaking the latch. In Chomsk, neighbors enter a house first and then greet the people they came to see, so their demands were not unusual. Rousing himself sleepily, Peter again spoke of the more perfect way — of repentance and faith in the Savior of the world, whom he had personally come to know. No matter how long he preached, they never tired of listening.

There were some who were not as patient. Devout Orthodox Russians objected to the evangelical message that Peter had brought to their village. They followed Peter from house to house as he led evangelistic meetings, throwing vegetables, even bricks and rocks, to show their hatred for the Gospel.

"I will show you what I think of this new religion," one young man cried. He seized a hymnbook and ran into the street, tearing out the pages and scattering them to the winds. "There!" he shouted. "Begone with your Gospel."

Two weeks later, that young man was dead of a mysterious cause. His death brought fear to the villagers. Peter's meetings were more popular than ever and hundreds of people opened their hearts to the Lord. God used the wrath of man to bring glory to His name.

Four Christian friends from a distant city arrived the second evening after they had received the news of Peter's return. They had been converted in St. Petersburg and were eager to talk to Peter about the faith they shared. The believers sang hymns for the people, adding to the excitement of the all-day meetings.

Services were scheduled in the village so more people could come to hear Peter preach. He discovered that some people would often walk up to 30 kilometers (almost 20 miles), then stand for hours until the service was over. They were not satisfied unless the meetings lasted at least three hours. Peter's heart was stirred with compassion for his people. He heard their prayers and saw the great hunger and openness as they drank in the story of redemption and applied it to their own lives.

Opposition to Peter's message came from an unexpected source — his mother and brother. Because he did not drink vodka and enjoy other worldly amusements, they were angry.

"I have no desire whatsoever for smoking, dancing, and drinking," Peter tried to explain. "Such things can displease the Lord. I only long to know more of God and to live wholly for Him."

Friends and relatives insisted that Peter stop preaching. They predicted that in a couple of weeks they would have him back into his old life of sin. They pressed Peter to buy drinks for them.

For 11 months the awkwardness continued, Peter's mother and brother urging him to forget his faith and be one of them again. Often he heard coarse language as he entered the house. Cursing would sometimes continue into the night. Andrei was so ashamed of his brother that he would not even walk with him through the village. His mother abandoned her pleas and would have little to do with her eldest son.

When Peter's life was threatened and his sanity seemed to be attacked, he prayed more earnestly that God would protect him and give him rest. "Anywhere with Jesus I can go to sleep," he repeated to himself many times, remembering the refrain of an old hymn. He was beginning to understand more fully the meaning of those wonderful words. He needed God's protection at night as well as during the day.

Friends in America occasionally sent funds to sustain Peter in his preaching. He used much of it to build a chapel where he could freely preach the Good News of God's grace. He bought shoes for the poor and bread for the hungry. He purchased roasted calves for $2 and a whole lamb for $1 so they could be served at special church suppers. Word traveled fast that the "rich American" was buying Christians for his chapel. His mother was angered and embarrassed by her son's tactics. "You should know better," she scolded.

But Peter was unable to stop. One day, near the Christmas season, a poor father rushed up to him on the street and asked for something to take to his children for Christmas. Peter bought him some white bread — a delicacy as welcome as cake to that community — and the father knelt right down in the mud on the street and thanked Peter.

A merchant found Peter alone one day and in a low voice asked. "How much does one have to pay to join your religion?"

"Nothing!" Peter replied.

"Nothing? You are lying!" the merchant demanded.

"No, I promise I am telling you the truth. I don't pay anybody to become a Christian."

"That's too bad," the merchant said, shaking his head. "I was thinking of joining your group."

Whenever anyone appeared on the street with a new pair of shoes, Peter's mother was convinced that her son had bought them with his American dollars. "Save your money, Pyotr!" she insisted. "You will need it when you get married."

Mrs. Deyneka was unsuccessful in stopping her generous son from helping the poor. Neither could she convince him to marry one of the girls she had selected for him.

"Just look at all the potatoes you could have had if you had married her!" his mother complained when he turned down her first choice. Of the second girl she announced happily, "Her father will give you a cow!"

"Please, Mama," Peter would object. "I don't want to marry potatoes, nor do I wish to marry a cow."

Peter had no plans to return to America. He only wanted to continue preaching in revival meetings among his people. They wanted to know the way to heaven — and Peter could tell them.

5

A BRIDE FOR PETER

Peter Deyneka had returned to his native Russia a single man, but he went back to America married to a quiet Russian girl from Borisovka whose spiritual zeal matched his own.

Six months before their wedding day, Vera Demidovich could not have imagined that she would one day travel to fabled America as the wife of an evangelist. She had suffered much from the madness of war and the scourge of famine. As the daughter of a schoolteacher and a part-time Russian Orthodox lay reader, she knew nothing of the saving grace of the Lord Jesus Christ.

The young girl who became a valued partner in Peter Deyneka's global ministries was born in a one-room home attached to a schoolhouse where her father taught arithmetic and grammar. There was just a table in the room with benches around the walls. Although Russian homes typically had dirt floors, the Demidovich residence had a modern wooden floor because it was part of the schoolhouse.

Her mother sang hymns and folk songs to Vera, her first-born child, and fed her gruel. Olga, a second daughter, was added as the years passed. The girls sewed pillows, embroidered tablecloths, and sang songs with their parents around the supper table.

The family spent summers on a four-acre plot of ground that yielded potatoes, lettuce, carrots, cucumbers, wheat, and some fruit. They also had cows. It was customary to walk the five miles to Gorodetz with farm crops to trade what the Demidoviches had produced for household needs.

Their small world was a community of relatives and friends within a 15-mile radius of Borisovka.

In 1914, the year Peter Deyneka left for America at the age of 15, Vera was eight. During the summer harvest that year, messengers announced that German army troops were advancing toward Borisovka. Vera found a small trunk and put all the precious possessions of her girlhood into it. Then she waited quietly for her father to take her away. While her sister Olga cried and complained about the ominous news, Vera sat patiently, her placid blue eyes taking in every detail.

Several days passed, then government officials rode at a gallop through the village, warning everyone that the German army would be upon them the following morning. Almost instantly, the roads were jammed with refugees fleeing eastward.

In addition to the scourge of war, the countryside was caught in the grip of a severe famine. Cattle were dying of thirst and crops were parched from lack of rainfall. Rivers had dried up and wells yielded the last drops to their desperate owners.

Mr. Demidovich packed as many vegetables and as much bread and salt pork as his family could carry, then led them to the nearest railroad depot. The last train had departed, but they found a horse and wagon whose owner had abandoned them to catch the train. They appropriated the horse and wagon and traveled 15 miles to another town, hoping and praying that another train would whisk them away from the advancing enemy soldiers.

The station was small and so was the train that stood waiting as the Demidovich family rolled up in the wagon.

"This is the last train to leave this area before the bridge is blown up," an official told them. "Get on if you can."

Railroad workers were swarming around the train, trying to find the best places to board. Some of the workers tried to keep the Demidovich family off. Many of the people had become hysterical with fear. Police managed to restore order, threatening to punish the railroad workers for keeping others off the train. "Do you think you are the only ones we are saving?" they asked.

Vera and her family squeezed into the cattle train with scant provisions — and no water. The train began to move, carrying its cargo of humanity away from the war front toward the interior of Russia. At night, fearing that children might fall out of the train while it was moving or that some weak and sickly people would be pushed out, officials nailed the train doors shut.

An epidemic of cholera swept the evacuees, taking a deadly toll among the people. The disease added a new dimension of misery to the thirsty travelers as the train rolled on. Officials spread lime on the floor of the train and on the platforms of each station they passed, trying to kill the germs of cholera. Many sick people were simply unloaded and left behind to die as the train relentlessly moved on. Vera's aunt, Natasha Leonovich, was so miserable she wished to die, and sat among the cholera victims hoping she would contract the disease. But death eluded her and her misery only increased.

The engine was a coal-burning locomotive which continually bathed the passengers with soot and heat. When coal ran out, the engineer would stop in forests where the weakened passengers would have to help cut down trees to provide fuel to keep the train going.

For nearly one month, the Demidovich family stayed on that train. Wounded soldiers were carried on and off as the train moved eastward. The government set up tables of food for soldiers at selected stations. Sometimes the passengers on the cramped train were allowed to join them and partake sparingly.

Finally, the rains descended. The train would stop at little streams from which the people could drink out of dishes, saucers, and cups — whatever they could find.

The depression of the passengers increased with each mile. They wept and sobbed almost constantly. Even the men cried in those desperate days of uncertainty and suffering. "What is going to happen to us?" they asked. No one had any idea where they were going or where they would eventually disembark.

Vera's aunt thought there was a general feeling among the Russian people on the train that they had offended God by their sins. They considered their anguish punishment for their iniquities. But there was no one among them to point beyond the traditions of the Russian Orthodox Church to forgiveness in Jesus Christ.

Vera's mother also cried much on the journey. She was not a stoic like her husband, and Vera was just like her dad. It seemed she had a temperament to endure hardships, whereas sister Olga was tempestuous and lively. While Olga was prone to outwardly complaining, Vera kept to herself and said very little.

A fellow teacher became acquainted with Vera's father. She invited his family to leave the train with her and settle in the city of Masalsk for the duration of the war. For one year, they lived in the home of that schoolteacher — just a day's ride from Moscow. Mr. Demidovich served as a Psalm reader in the Orthodox Church while Mrs. Demidovich sewed for the people in the village.

From Masalsk, they eventually moved southward to the Crimea and the Caucasus near the Black Sea, remaining there for two years. As the war began to wind down, their hearts turned back to White Russia and they made plans to move home. Unfortunately it was now 3,000 miles away, but they were determined to go.

Mr. Demidovich traded some valuables for a horse that would assist him and his family in the long journey. They loaded their few possessions onto a cart and began the 3,000-mile trek back to their home village — walking alongside the cart as the horse plodded westward, leading them to a new life and a new beginning. Walking was their only mode of travel since other forms of transportation had been knocked out during the war. It also hadn't rained for two years and famine was again a killer, so their thoughts were usually consumed with finding enough food to stay alive.

They left the Crimea in the heat of summer, but it was snowing in Borisovka when they arrived. Their house had been destroyed, so they lived for a time with a grandfather and an uncle. They also discovered that the Polish-Russian border had changed so that their village was now in Poland. This meant Vera's father was no longer licensed to teach school and Russian was not the official language of Borisovka anymore.

They eventually settled on a bit of land Mr. Demidovich's father had left him, and they planted a new crop for a new season. Vera helped work the farm, and she sometimes walked 40 miles to visit relatives and friends. In one of the villages she visited after one of these 40-mile treks, she heard that a Russian evangelist had come to conduct Gospel services. He had migrated to Canada, but out of concern for the spiritual needs of his own people he had returned to Russia. Relatives took Vera along to a house meeting to hear the man and his teachings.

Some 20 people gathered in the small house that day. The Canadian immigrant and another man were the only two Christians in the entire community. As Vera listened to the message of God's redeeming love, her heart was strangely moved. Eagerly, she joined the others who committed their lives to Jesus Christ. She would never be the same again.

Later, Vera's sister and mother arrived in the same village to visit relatives. She took them to hear the evangelists, but her family did not like what they heard. They returned home divided by the Sword of Truth. After that, Vera had to quietly sneak out of the house very early in the morning so she would not be hindered in her walk to the nearest church services 12 miles away.

Three years later, Peter Deyneka came to that same village to preach. Vera Demidovich had endured hardship as a good soldier of Jesus Christ and had earned a noble reputation among the congregation. Peter, too, was impressed by the 20-year-old girl's devotion to her Lord. After they were introduced, a bond of friendship cemented their future. Both became convinced that God had brought them together to continue His work as man and wife. Six months after their meeting, Vera Demidovich and Peter Deyneka were married on May 23, 1926.

According to the Russian Orthodox traditions and customs at that time, the couple to be married would walk in a circle three times behind the priest. Other traditional customs accompanied the Orthodox ritual, but villagers who knew Vera and Peter were certain they would arrange an evangelical wedding.

On the big day, large crowds gathered early in the morning both at the little chapel in Peter's native village of Chomsk and in the Demidovich home 15 miles away. Of course Peter took advantage of the occasion to preach the Gospel, first at the home of his bride and later at the evangelical church in Chomsk.

A light lunch of black bread and Russian tea was served in Vera's home. From there, the couple rode in separate wagons to the chapel in Chomsk for the ceremony. Many young people rode along in the wagons, singing as they bumped along on the dirt roads.

It was 3:00 in the afternoon when they finally arrived at Chomsk to greet the large crowds of waiting people. The scene reminded Peter of market day. Four policemen scurried around to keep order among the Russians, Jews, and Poles who had come to witness the wedding ceremony of evangelical Christians.

A choir in the chapel began singing *Crown Him!*, followed by other songs appropriate for the occasion. A Russian Christian missionary who had also been to America was conveniently on hand to officiate the wedding.

After the simple ceremony, the crowd moved en masse to the house of Peter's mother where they enjoyed a rare treat — roast veal with black bread and Russian tea. The singing continued like a benediction on the happy couple, and the sun had long since disappeared when the singing and the preaching came to an end on that momentous day.

"We had honey, but no moon!" Peter told friends in America when he described the rainy days that followed. He and Vera desired more than anything else to put the Lord's work ahead of their own comfort, so the next morning they traveled on foot in pouring rain for 16 miles to the homes of Vera's relatives to distribute Gospel portions and tell them about Jesus Christ. When they arrived, they found that a crowd of eager people had already gathered. They would not even let the bride and groom dry their clothes. They had to begin the services immediately.

Peter preached until 1:00, thinking that would suffice. "You're not going to go after just a two-hour service!" exclaimed one mother with a six-month-old baby. "I walked 20 miles to this place to hear God's Word, and you want to quit so soon?"

There was nothing to do but have a short recess and continue with another service, lasting until 5:00 p.m.

The newlyweds stayed the night with relatives. In the morning the rain poured down again, but they set their course toward a village 12 miles away through the woods. They borrowed a team of horses and a horse blanket to cover their heads. Before they arrived, however, the blanket had become soaked and dirt had begun to trickle down their faces.

"In the afternoon we reached the village where a crowd was waiting for us," Peter wrote. "We had a wonderful Gospel service, even though we were dirty, cold, and tired. It was a great encouragement to be able to witness for the Lord."

They were supremely happy doing the work of the Lord on their honeymoon, and a spirit of revival followed them. Russian people eagerly responded to the message of salvation and believers were stirred in their zeal to follow the Lord more closely.

For Peter, the days of his honeymoon marked the end of a long and torturous sojourn with his unbelieving family. Close friends urged him to return to the United States, where he might find his health again and secure the support of Christian people in America for the Russian work. But since documents would need to be acquired for Vera, he would have to go ahead without her. He would also have to stop at the American consulate in Warsaw, Poland, where he would need to prove he had enough money to care for his wife when she arrived in the United States.

A tearful farewell followed in Peter's home, where many skeptics gathered with the Christians. His mother and brother had not yet come to the Lord and they opposed his going. But at 5:00 the following morning, he set his face once again toward America for the momentous events that would change the course of his life.

6

BLAZING NEW TRAILS

As Peter sailed into New York's harbor once again, past the Statue of Liberty where many of his countrymen were being processed as immigrants, his mind was fixed on the many fond memories of his homeland. At the forefront of his thoughts was his devoted new bride, who patiently waited back in Russia for the ticket that he would send to her just as soon as possible.

Peter also thought of his Russian brethren whom he had left behind. Many were willing to give themselves fully to the preaching of the Gospel, but they had no funds. *Willing hearts, but no means of support,* Peter mused as he stood at the rail of the ocean liner and gazed eastward. Mentally, he took an account of his resources. He had nothing — nothing but the riches of Christ Jesus, which were multiplied as willing people invested in the outreach of the Gospel.

"I have seen the vision," he told Russian friends in New York City. "I have heard their cries. I cannot forget my people."

In the midsummer heat of New York, Peter began at once to seek out fellow believers among Russians to share with them his needs and burdens. They were excited and inspired by what he had to say, and they eagerly invited him to conduct meetings and conferences where he could speak of their brothers and sisters in the homeland and report on the revival meetings he had led across the sea.

Rev. Ivan Stepanovich Prokhanov, a Russian from St. Petersburg (formerly Leningrad), was the principal speaker in one of those conferences.

He was an engineer whose heart had been captured by the Savior and set afire for evangelism. Prokhanov was a mountain of a man and had been sent to the United States the first time by the Westinghouse Company, at whose branch office he was employed in Russia. Now, as president of the All-Russian Evangelical Christian Union headquartered in St. Petersburg, the missionary statesman had returned to North America to raise funds for that ministry. He arrived in New York on May 23, 1925, and stayed until November 1926, just long enough to meet Peter Deyneka and join forces with him.

A severe hunger for Bibles in Russia had prompted Prokhanov's return to America. He negotiated with Christian friends who booked meetings for him in American churches. Peter Deyneka traveled with him, visiting churches all over the United States. The Lord answered prayer and provided in amazing ways, and together they raised a total of $100,000 for Russian Bibles.

Common goals and concerns drew the two men closer together. On November 1, 1926, at Prokhanov's request, Peter Deyneka was appointed field secretary and traveling Russian evangelist of the Evangelical Christian Union. His duties were to raise funds for evangelistic work in Russia, speaking both in Russian and English churches across the United States and Canada.

Six weeks after her husband's appointment with the Evangelical Christian Union, Mrs. Deyneka arrived from Russia. As quickly as they could make the necessary arrangements, the couple left for Chicago, the city where Peter had found the Lord. This was his home in America, and it would also serve well as a centrally located base for his ministry.

"During those early years, I traveled all of the time throughout the United States and Canada," Peter recalled, "conducting evangelistic meetings, speaking at missionary conventions and youth rallies, and filling the pulpits of various churches. I had the joy of seeing hundreds of people accept the Lord Jesus Christ as their Savior, and I saw hundreds more volunteer for Christian service."

Peter's ministry with the Evangelical Christian Union occupied nearly all his waking hours. He had been so busy when his wife arrived from Russia that he had neglected to have a wedding picture taken. Upon hearing this, Mr. and Mrs. Steven Tovstenko, Peter's friends in Minneapolis when he had attended Bible school in St. Paul, invited Peter and Vera for a visit and arranged for a wedding picture. Mrs. Tovstenko helped Vera dress for the official photographic record of their wedding, even though the event had occurred half a world away and half a year past.

—→•——⊨◇⊨——•←—

As funds from America began flowing into Russia in the 1920s, the All-Russian Evangelical Christian Union gathered strength for its various ministries. Rev. Prokhanov used his enormous influence among Christians and non-Christians alike to advance the cause of Christ in a nation that was officially atheistic.

One of the most vital needs in Russia was for Bibles, Christian literature, and hymnbooks. Prokhanov had earlier approached the Czarist Ministry of the Interior in St. Petersburg, requesting that its printing office furnish hymnbooks for the evangelical churches. This same department of the government had decreed in the early 1900s that evangelicals were "dangerous to church and State activities, therefore their right to assemble for services is prohibited."

In 1901, a governmental decree directed that no religious literature could be distributed except that which was authorized by the official government printing division — the Orthodox Church. Nevertheless, Prokhanov knew that its printing department was eager for business. Needless to say, the planned approach by the evangelical leader caused the evangelical church apprehension.

"Don't try it!" his friends warned. "It's impossible!"

But Prokhanov would not be deterred. He felt a strong assurance that God would turn what man had intended for evil into an opportunity to bring glory to His name. With the manuscript for a new hymnal under his arm, Prokhanov approached the director of the printing bureau of the Ministry of the Interior.

"I wish to place an order for a hymnbook," he said.

The official studied the title — *Gusli* (The Harps). He did not know that the manuscript contained hymns used in Gospel meetings.

"How many copies do you want?" the director asked.

"I need 20,000," Prokhanov stated, "and I would like to have the whole quantity printed as quickly as possible."

The printer made some notes. "All right, we'll push the job," he promised. "And you don't need to worry about the approval of the censors. We'll take care of it."

Prokhanov left the department smiling. "Here I had been worried about the censors, trying so hard to figure out how to cross that bridge," he later explained to friends, "only to find out that the bridge was not even there!"

In 90 days, the entire edition (20,000 copies) of *Gusli* was delivered. Believers bought them quickly, afraid that government or Orthodox Church officials might discover the new evangelical publication and clamp down on the inventory.

The Christians could scarcely believe what they now held in their hands. The edict against the publishing of any religious literature was well known. Yet right there in the front of the book was the imprimatur of the government: "Printed in the printing establishment of the Ministry of the Interior, St. Petersburg."

The years of 1922 to 1928 marked history's fastest expansion of the Gospel in Russian history. Leading this movement was the publishing of Bibles and hymnbooks. The Russian people were starved for copies of the Word of God.

During this period of great evangelistic opportunity, the 1923 Lenin Constitution was in effect which allowed both religion and antireligion the right to propagandize. This meant that Christians not only had opportunity to print Gospel literature, but also to preach the Gospel — even outside churches.

But the Lenin constitution was changed by Stalin, and most articles of the Stalin Constitution were the ones that were enforced throughout the former Soviet Union. Article 124 of the Stalin Constitution reads: "In order to assure to citizens freedom of conscience, the church in the U.S.S.R. is separated from the State, and the school from the church. Freedom of religious worship and freedom of antireligious propaganda is recognized for all citizens."

In reality, Stalin's constitution meant that while atheism could be freely propagated, religious worship was officially curtailed to registered church buildings.

During the 1920s, Prokhanov organized *The Christian* magazine. Even though 15,000 copies were distributed each month, the evangelist impatiently referred to it as "an insufficient supply." Such publishing enterprises were not forbidden in the Soviet Union at that time. However, believers were hindered during those years of opportunity due to shortages of paper and lack of funding.

"It was very sad," Prokhanov wrote. "People everywhere were asking for Bibles, but we could not supply them." In many places, peasants offered a cow or a sack of precious grain in exchange for one Bible.

From December 1926 through May 1928, Russian Christians were able to print the following:

Bibles	35,000
New Testaments	25,000
Hymnals	
The Gospel Songs	25,000
Spiritual Songs	25,000
the above, with notes	10,000
Bible Concordances	15,000
The Gospel Advisor (a church calendar	
read repeatedly throughout the year)	40,000
Total publications:	175,000

From 1914 to 1957, this was the *only* Scripture allowed to be printed on the presses of the Russian government. Prokhanov calls it "a gift from God and the American Christians to the Russian people." The deep significance of this production and distribution of the Word of God across Russia is best understood and appreciated when one remembers that during this famine of Scripture the whole of Russia was continually being bombarded with atheistic propaganda.

━┿━ ⊨◇⊐ ━┿━

At the beginning of 1930, Rev. Prokhanov invited Peter to return to White Russia and take advantage of the partially open doors for evangelism. The Deynekas' first child, Ruth, had been born by then, but both parents were willing for Peter to return to his people and continue his ministry. On February 22, 1930, Peter left for his homeland aboard the *S.S. Majestic* accompanied by A. R. Scherling, a Christian businessman from Fargo, North Dakota.

A series of meetings led the two Americans to Riga, Latvia, where they found people anxiously waiting for them. They intended to close their services by noon, but the audiences would weep and plead for them to continue. In the evenings, they would return for more evangelistic services. The Gospel hall would again be overflowing with eager listeners. The Spirit of the Lord was poured out mightily. A touch of revival inspired them, renewing their zeal to press on in the work.

From Riga they traveled through a blizzard to Tartu, Estonia, fully expecting their meeting to be canceled. But the hall was filled with Russians and Germans. Again, the Holy Spirit awakened believers and brought conviction on the assembled citizens.

"We have no time for rest," Peter wrote. "They tell us we can rest at the next place. But at the next place, they tell us the same thing. Now they are telling us we can rest when we return to America!"

At each meeting in the satellite countries — Poland, Latvia, Czechoslovakia, Yugoslavia — they prayed for the suffering Christians in Russia.

When they entered White Russia, Peter grew homesick to see his mother, even though she had told him four years earlier to never come back. Undeterred, Peter was determined to see her.

As the men arrived by horse and wagon in the little town of Chomsk, Peter's mother saw him through the window and rushed out to meet him, even before he got off the wagon.

"My dear son!" she cried out. "I gave my heart to the Lord, and God has made me a new creature! Now I will be a different mother to you."

Peter could hardly believe it. Weeping, he exclaimed, "My prayers have been answered!"

At the meeting that evening, Peter's mother stood up and told her neighbors and friends, "I persecuted my son because I was in spiritual darkness and did not know the Lord, but now I have given myself to God. I want to live for Him." That same week, she was baptized in the very same river from which her late fisherman husband had made a living.

In 1930, the evangelical church in Russia numbered nearly three million believers. Meetings often lasted for three hours. People everywhere clamored to hear what the Bible taught. It was not uncommon to hear of Jewish people being converted to Christ, and the fanaticism of Islam was so tempered that in some parts of Russia the Muslims actually invited evangelical preachers to speak about Jesus Christ in their mosques.

But it was at this time that opportunities and freedom for evangelism came to an abrupt halt. The constitution of 1929 was amended to give antireligious propaganda more privileges and to deny the same to religion — no more open preaching and evangelism. But the fruitful years had drawn countless thousands into the kingdom of God.

"The wonderful progress of the Gospel in my country during the years of 1924 to 1930 amounted to a national Gospel reformation," Peter observed. "All classes of Russian people — all nationalities, tribes, and occupations — were caught up in a sweeping revival. This was a specific answer to prayer. It was a miracle during a time after the Revolution when atheism officially controlled the government."

The official government magazine *The Atheist* often ran caricatures of the evangelicals, but this strategy backfired on the editors. So many readers were curious about the Christians that they sent letters asking for Christian literature to find out who they were. "In this way," a pastor wrote, "even atheism helped us spread the Gospel. It was good advertising for the moment and led to a source of new converts."

The atheists were fond of arranging "antireligious debates" in the largest halls, and the rooms would always be filled. Usually the first speakers railed against God, religion, and moral law. Afterward, the defenders of religion were allowed to speak. It is clear from Rev. Prokhanov's records that audiences would typically interrupt the evangelical speakers to ask for the addresses of churches. As a result, new hearers filled the humble sanctuaries of Russian believers following the well-publicized debates.

Religious bodies sometimes distrusted each other. But when the atheists came with their propaganda, all the various denominations and groups solidly united to fight back.

"The hearts of the Russian people and their hunger for God could not accept the atheistic doctrine," Prokhanov wrote. "On the one hand, they were disappointed in the old system of the Orthodox Church. On the other hand, they had no desire to accept the new system of atheism."

Peter Deyneka did not realize that his trip to White Russia in 1930 would be his last opportunity to freely preach to the people of Russia. But there would be other ways and other workers. It was time in God's scheme for an organization that would evangelize the Russian people, both in their own country and to the farthest reaches of the earth.

7

A MISSION IS BORN

Adverse winds in the early 1930s blew shut the doors of evangelistic opportunity in the former Soviet Union. Millions of citizens chose to vote against the militant atheistic society of Russia by fleeing to other parts of the world. It was the only vote they had.

In June 1931, Peter resigned as field secretary and traveling missionary for Prokhanov's All-Russian Evangelical Christian Union and joined Pastor Paul Rader's missionary society based at Chicago Gospel Tabernacle. Rader, Peter's spiritual father and mentor, had repeatedly urged the young Russian to join his staff and assist in missionary rallies. Peter seized the opportunity to burden American Christians who could help evangelize Slavic people.

On July 1, 1931, Peter became secretary of the Russian work on behalf of Rader's World-Wide Christian Couriers. The concept for the World-Wide Christian Couriers was to establish neighborhood Bible classes by Christian people in the homes of unbelievers. The believers would bring in others and then introduce them to Christ. It was purely home evangelism, and Paul Rader envisioned the concept circling the globe.

Occasionally Peter would arrange conventions, bringing together "courier classes" in large gatherings called *tamasha*. The word was adapted from an undisclosed foreign language to describe large gatherings of people. The programs were rather innovative for the time and featured class manuals, coins with insignia on them, music and banners, and a variety of special speakers.

Rader launched the first Christian radio broadcast in the Chicago area. He also kept up quite a hectic itinerary of meetings and Bible conferences to occupy the long hours and days of his hard-driving ministry. The Rader-sponsored programs gave Peter numerous opportunities to expose believers to the needs of Russian Christians. Rader always put Peter in charge of prayer meetings — seasons of intercession which often lasted the entire night.

From Ivan Prokhanov, Peter learned what God can do through a Russian with organizational abilities. Paul Rader taught Peter how to pray and how to powerfully preach with anecdotes and stories to illustrate truth and create spiritual hunger. Two different men of God who had profound influence on Peter's life, helped prepare him for what God had in store.

━┼━ ⊞◊⊟ ┼━

In September 1933, a cable summoned Peter to Slavic countries in Eastern Europe for another extensive tour sponsored by the Union of Slavic Churches of Evangelical Christians in Poland. The meeting halls were packed, the services long, and the spiritual hunger intense.

Later that year, Peter returned from his third trip to Eastern Europe and Russia more convinced than ever that an agency was needed to exhort the people of North America to pray for the Slavic people — people to whom Peter had been divinely appointed as a missionary. At first he fought the idea of establishing a new missionary organization. His administrative talent was untested. All he really knew how to do was to call people to prayer and repentance. God would have to do the rest.

For three days, Peter and his wife prayed and fasted, trying to determine whether the divine light was green or red in the matter of establishing a mission. They paced up and down in their apartment, crying and praying — not forgetting to praise and thank the Lord for the answer they knew would come.

Peter went to see a prominent Christian businessman to ask him to join with him in establishing a mission to Slavic people.

"Do you have capital, Brother Peter?" the man wanted to know. "Any time you start an organization, you've got to have money!"

"Well, we don't have money, but we have God," Peter replied.

"Then I'll pray for you because I respect you, but I don't think I should join you," the businessman decided.

Outside, a winter rain began to fall. Peter was discouraged. To add to his discouragement, he got lost taking the wrong streetcar home. When he finally reached his apartment, his wife excitedly held up an envelope. "It's a letter from Iowa," she said.

Peter tore it open and found a check inside for $950 with a note from two elderly ladies: "Dear Peter: We met you a few years ago and we remember how you told us of your desire to preach the Gospel to the Russians. We are enclosing a check to help you do that."

Peter was so excited he immediately phoned the businessman.

"Is that all?" the voice on the other end of the line asked.

"Yes! Praise the Lord!" Peter exclaimed.

"What do you want me to do?"

"Well, nothing. I just wanted to give you this report," Peter replied.

That man missed an opportunity to participate in a miracle, but Peter was not without other supporters.

One afternoon while visiting with Paul Rood, pastor of Chicago's Lake View Mission Covenant Church, later to become president of the Bible Institute of Los Angeles (Biola University), Peter shared with his friend his burden to organize a missionary outreach among Slavic people around the world. Dr. Rood suggested they kneel in prayer and commit the matter to God. As they rose from their knees, Charles Bodeen walked in to discuss a matter with his pastor.

"Brother Charlie," Dr. Rood said, "Peter has a great burden to evangelize Russians, and we're going to help him."

The three men put their arms around each other, and in that informal circle once again lifted their hearts to God in prayer. The date was set for a committee meeting, one week later.

On January 6, 1934, five men assembled in the back room of C. B. Hedstrom's shoe store on Belmont Avenue near Clark Street. The afternoon weather that Saturday was cold, accented by a chill wind blowing in off Lake Michigan. At that original committee meeting with Peter were Dr. Rood, C. B. Hedstrom, Dr. Arthur Brown (a surgeon), and George Benson (a businessman).

The name they chose was the Russian Gospel Association, later renamed Slavic Gospel Association. Dr. Rood was elected chairman of the board, George Benson became the secretary-treasurer, Arthur Brown and C. B. Hedstrom were members of the executive committee, and Peter Deyneka was named general director and missionary evangelist.

The die was cast. The organization became the lengthened shadow of the "rushing Russian" and was on its way to becoming the largest mission of its kind in the world.

In his first letter to prospective supporters, Paul Rood wrote . . .

> Peter Deyneka is a native Russian Christian who is on the firing line for God. He has a vision and a passion for the evangelization of his people. A group of us who devoutly believe in Brother Deyneka's sincerity and genuineness have gladly associated ourselves with him to help realize his vision.
>
> Christ died for the Russians as well as for all other nationalities. Multitudes among the Russians are responsive to the Gospel and many are being saved. The field in which our association is working is white unto harvest. Christ is coming, and the time is short. What is going to be done will have to be done soon. We ask for your prayers.

The first gifts came from the board members themselves. Gradually, the base of support was broadened by adding friends that Peter Deyneka had made during previous years of ministry, eventually expanding to include churches and individuals across the United States and Canada.

✦━ ❧❖❧ ━✦

Peter and Vera Deyneka carefully groomed their children to take part in the work to which God had called them. When Ruth was just three years old, she touched her father's heart by her strong desire to be near him. One evening while his wife was caring for household matters, Peter was packing his suitcase to leave for a speaking engagement. But Ruthie got hold of his luggage and hung on. "No, Papa!" she cried. "I won't let you go! I won't let you go!"

Peter recalled the moment with tears, "I had to jerk my suitcase out of her hands; she wouldn't let me go. It nearly broke my heart. I could hear her a block away crying and calling out for me. I was crying too. It was not easy. My wife cried many times as well, but when you say 'Yes' to Jesus, you have to go — you have to pay the price."

Ruth was given piano lessons and taught to sing and speak in the Russian language. Second-born Peter Jr. was also made to take Russian and piano lessons, even when he grumbled and complained. "Piano is for girls," he mumbled to his father one day, tears running down his face.

Since Peter had enjoyed little childhood leisure in Russian village life, he sometimes found it rather difficult to understand his own son's desire to play baseball and shoot marbles. "The Bible says, 'Marble not!'" he once told Peter Jr., providing a unique interpretation of the familiar text.

When the Deynekas' third and last child, Lydia, was only five years old, she crawled upon her father's knees one evening and said, "Daddy, when are we going for a ride? Other children go."

Peter replied, "I have no time to take you now, but on Sunday evening I'll take you with me."

The day came and it was bitter cold. "I want to go with Daddy!" she reminded her mother.

That evening she sat in the service and listened to her father preach. When Peter gave the invitation and people began to come forward, two ladies approached on his right and Lydia on his left.

"I am going to kneel down first with my daughter," Peter told the congregation. "Lydia, do you want something from the Lord?"

"Yes, Papa. I want Jesus to come into my heart and make me a Christian girl."

Peter prayed with her, thrilled that he had the privilege of sharing this special occasion with his youngest child — the moment when she was made a new creature in Jesus Christ.

In the summer months, when the children weren't in school, Peter arranged his schedule so that he could take all of them with him on his travels. He taught them to sing choruses and participate in the meetings, faithfully preparing the children to serve Christ. Despite protests that "we are American now, Papa," all three children had lessons in the Russian language so they would be better equipped to minister to Slavic people.

Not an evening passed without family prayers. When they were in high school, the children knew they could not leave the house for evening activities until after prayer, so they would sometimes hurry their parents to start the prayer time.

Mrs. Deyneka was a truly faithful wife, doing whatever was necessary to keep the house in order. When they lived in a third-story apartment in Chicago, she walked up and down several flights of stairs to carry coal from the basement to heat the stove. She also played a large role in raising godly children. While Peter traveled, she remained at home with the little ones. She fasted every Friday and kept the children diligent in their schoolwork and their prayers, instilling in them and nurturing the notion of full-time Christian service. She stayed at home for more than 40 years, not traveling with Peter until after their first grandchild was born.

✦—✦ ⚏◈⚎ ✦—✦

The mission grew steadily. When Peter ran into administrative problems, he depended on the dynamism of prayer and faith. Once each month he hung a sign on the door of his office (which was in his home) announcing a day of prayer. No one was allowed to disturb the staff that day because they were giving the entire day to prayer. Those prayers watered the soil of every preaching mission.

Wherever Peter traveled, people responded to his message. Christians found the courage to surrender their talents and resources to God. The unsaved were moved to respond to God's saving grace. People who had forgotten the needs of missions were drawn into the widening circle of staunch supporters.

As Peter traveled out from his Chicago hub, he took other young people with him. Among those early team members were Walter Covich, a Chicagoan of Russian descent who taught Peter how to drive a car and who later established a work among Russians in Alaska; Const and Elizabeth Lewshenia, who became active in ministries in South America; Mary Fewchuk, who with her husband Sam served as missionaries in South America and Australia; and Andrew Semenchuk, who was later to become the director of the mission's Russian Bible school in Argentina.

The mission's first year passed swiftly. On January 11, 1935, they celebrated that first milestone with a missionary rally at Lake View Mission Covenant Church in Chicago. The celebration lasted all day, beginning at 10:30 a.m. with an opening prayer by Rev. Emil Burke, an advisory member. C. B. Hedstrom, vice chairman of SGA, presided. Music was provided by Mr. and Mrs. E. Plunkett. Afterward, SGA chairman Dr. Paul Rood introduced Dr. Harry Ironside, then pastor of Moody Memorial Church. Peter closed this session with a brief address on *Why Evangelize the Russians*, followed by a time of prayer.

At 2:30 p.m. the second session opened, this time featuring a message by Dr. Bob Jones, president of Bob Jones College in Cleveland, Tennessee. Dr. Jones had just returned from a missionary trip to Russia. A third session opened at 7:30 p.m. with Dr. Jones preaching again, stressing how hungry the Russian people were for the Gospel. He had seen many hundreds stand for nine hours in one day, listening to the Gospel.

The day's events ended at 10:15 p.m. When the crowds had gone and the offering had been counted, the executive committee and their wives knelt down in the middle of that auditorium and cried a thankful prayer to God for a most wonderful first anniversary celebration.

8

ONE MESSAGE FOR ONE WORLD

The executive committee of the newly formed Slavic Gospel Association strongly believed in sending financial support to areas of greatest need, but only through the advice and supervision of seasoned Christian leaders in those areas. This policy required that Peter travel almost constantly in the early days to fields where Slavic missionaries labored and where pastors and evangelists were in short supply. He never traveled on purely administrative assignments. He always combined them with evangelistic meetings, and he always preached. In due time, the fruits of righteousness always followed.

People often wondered if Peter was ever inspirationally "dry" before a meeting. "Dry? Oh, yes! Sometimes I feel like I don't know what I'm going to say even as the last hymn is being sung and I'm being introduced. But then God gives me a message and I start in."

In 1937, Peter embarked on an extended journey to the Soviet Union, a journey which eventually took him around the world. Travel funds were supplied separately so that nothing was taken from SGA's general fund or missionary reserve.

The board of directors urged Peter to investigate the situation in his homeland one more time, even though they recognized the dangers. Hitler's blitzkrieg against Poland was only two years away. Rumors of war were increasing. Pressure against most citizens in Stalin's Russia was by now intense, yet reports indicated that the Christian faith was alive and vital. Many Christian leaders were being sent to the vast region of Siberia.

This journey to Russia was Peter's fourth as an evangelist. Some urged him not to go because of the dangers, but he left Chicago on March 22, his ticket having been purchased by interested friends for this preaching and fact-finding journey. He also left with the blessing of his brave wife, Vera, who could not help knowing the dangers her husband faced.

Peter sailed from New York on the *R.M.S. Queen Mary* and reached France in four days. He stood out prominently on voyages such as this one and was usually tapped by the ship's authorities to lead worship services. Out of those casual meetings at sea came lasting friendships and faithful financial supporters of the mission.

Peter disembarked at Cherbourg and took a train for Paris. Letters ahead of the trip had arranged a meeting with Russian believers at a Gospel hall rented for their services. He continued on to Geneva . . . Rome . . . then Yugoslavia and through the city of Trieste, finding Russian communities everywhere. The basic themes in his meetings were deeper spiritual life, revival, and consecration.

From Belgrade, Yugoslavia, Peter traveled to Kishinev, arriving just after 3:00 a.m., to be met by two Messianic Jews who were missionaries among their people in this former Romanian capital. The Jewish brethren took him to various parts of the city on preaching missions. Through this contact, SGA had a continuing part in efforts to evangelize the Slavs of that city.

Peter's traveling companions throughout the years recall his absolute insistence on being half an hour early for every train, plane, or meeting. "I like to leave early in case we have a flat tire or get lost," he would say, even though he only had one flat tire in over 50 years of traveling. "That tire exploded so loudly it scared us inside the car."

From Kishinev, Peter journeyed to Rovno, Poland, two years ahead of the horrific Nazi blitzkriegs. He was met by Rev. A. Nichiporuk, a pastor-missionary in charge of a large Gospel church.

"The Holy Spirit so moved the hearts of people that many souls were saved and believers revived," Peter wrote following his ministry in Poland. The evangelistic success was all the more remarkable because the city was pelted by driving rain during his entire visit. Bad road conditions developed, but that could not hinder the gathering crowds.

Kowel was the next stop for the traveling missionary, and then Warsaw, where Peter boarded a train that would carry him to the border of Russia and home to Chomsk. The moment of parting always broke Peter's heart. Believers were grieved to see him go, strongly warning him not to travel eastward.

"But I *must* go," Peter replied to them, just as he had done to friends in America who had tried to dissuade him. They countered with dire predictions that the moment he stepped over the border the Bolsheviks would arrest him and offer him no way of escape.

"Don't take your Bible!" they advised. "If the Bolsheviks discover you are a Christian, they will surely put you in prison."

To each warning Peter simply replied that God was able to protect him from all dangers, and he set his face like a flint to enter his native land.

One Polish man in particular grieved for Peter and his family in America. "I am very burdened for you, Peter," he said repeatedly. "You will have a difficult time getting out of Russia."

Peter looked at him carefully. "Will you pray for me as I go?" he asked.

"Yes," the man promised, "but that will not help."

Peter smiled. *Some encouragement,* he thought.

Christian workers gathered late at night at the Warsaw train depot to see him off and to pray for his safety. They laid their hands on him, committing him to the Lord's care.

The train was filled with Russians and Poles traveling to the last Polish station of Zdowhonovo. Peter rode all night, arriving at the border town at eight the following morning. All the other passengers left the train at Zdowhonovo, leaving him completely alone in the coach.

Feelings of fear and loneliness gripped him. "I recalled all the warnings and advice my friends had given me just the day before," he said as he recalled the harrowing trip. "My thoughts wandered back to America and to my family. Would I see them again?"

At last the train began to move again, gaining speed rapidly. He crossed a beautiful land with an abundance of grain, fruit trees, and fertile vegetable farms. Everything was brightly illuminated by the gleaming rays of a golden morning sun. Each mile carried him nearer and nearer to the Soviet border.

As the train sped eastward, Peter watched the level terrain change. Along the railroad tracks grew verdant forests, sometimes stretching away in the distance as far as the eye could see. As he gazed out the window, he pondered seeing his mother again. Having received the Lord as her Savior in 1930, her greeting this time should be far different from the weeping and angry tirades that characterized her actions during his first visit home in 1925.

As the train approached the border, Peter found joy in the promises of God. "They were my only source of comfort," he said. "I could hear them echo through my heart one after another: *Have faith in God . . . Only believe . . . I am with you . . . I will never leave you or forsake you . . . Call to Me, and I will answer you, and show you great and mighty things, which you do not know.*"

As he peered through the open windows of the train, Peter saw in the distance two high posts marking the Russian gateway across the border. The train began to slow down. Peter lifted his trembling heart to God in prayer, resolving in his heart that he would not fear what man would do to him. "My Bible shall go with me!" he decided.

Soviet Russia! All the doors and windows in the train were abruptly closed and it became hot and stuffy. A Soviet officer stepped inside Peter's car and called, "Pozhalusta vash passport [passport, please]."

Peter fished into his pocket and drew out the precious document. The officer took it, saying, "You will get it back at Shepetovka" (the Russian customs house).

An hour later, the train pulled in to the customs house where an Intourist interpreter who knew English spoke to Peter in Russian. Almost immediately, a militia man and woman ordered him to open his suitcase. Peter obliged — and the first thing that fell out was his Bible. With trembling hands, he picked it up and handed it to the customs officer. The official looked it over and laid it aside, inspecting more closely other items in the luggage.

"Close it up," the inspector said.

Hallelujah! Peter sang in his heart. *My Bible is going with me!*

The woman officer counted his money and gave him a receipt. She also registered the camera with his passport. "You must show this receipt when you leave the country," she explained. "Without it, you will not be allowed to take your money out of Russia."

By 2:00 p.m., Peter was processed and ready to enter the country. The midsummer heat was almost unbearable, but Peter noticed he was shivering from fear. The year was 1937, and Russia was still in the murderous grip of Stalin's purges.

A few moments after repacking his suitcase, Peter was speeding southward on an express train toward Baku. In the dining car, he ate his first meal in Soviet Russia — a bowl of Ukrainian borscht, several slices of bread with butter, and a bottle of lemonade.

While Peter was still inside the train at the Kiev depot, a Russian Jew working for Intourist picked up his luggage and greeted him by name. The stranger announced he would be his guide during his stopover. A car was waiting at the station which took Peter directly to a hotel in the large city. As a tourist, Peter was treated to an exceptionally delicious supper. He noticed that the streets were clean, that clothing was expensive, and that the people were dressed simply but neatly.

On Sunday morning Peter wanted to find a Russian Gospel church, but his guide desired to take him to a shoe factory.

"We have plenty of shoes in America," Peter told his guide. "I am interested in seeing churches."

The guide boasted that "a good many" churches were open in Kiev. He did not think Peter would have difficulty finding one. "Go ahead and try to find one if you want to go to church to say your prayers."

"I could say my prayers in the hotel room," Peter replied, "but I want to see how the people worship in Protestant churches as well as in the Orthodox churches."

"Why?" the guide demanded. "Are you interested in religion?"

"Yes," Peter explained. "I believe in the Bible. I also believe in the Lord Jesus Christ as my Savior."

The guide shrugged.

Peter searched in vain for a church that Sunday morning. In his pocket he had the addresses of some Christian brethren, so he visited them instead. Through this contact, he found a Gospel church.

Peter noticed that several ministers were seated on the platform that evening. They appeared to be very poor and very thin, for indeed some had recently returned from years of exile.

One of the preachers stood up to greet the congregation. "Dear brothers and sisters, let us thank God for this wonderful opportunity we have to get together once more to worship our Lord Jesus Christ," the pastor said. "He is worthy of our praise. Let us pray."

Many in the room knelt. Others remained standing, as is the custom in Russian evangelical churches. With one voice, the Christians opened their hearts and prayed. The intercession continued for 15 minutes. Tears ran down the faces of many as they thanked God for the privilege of speaking to Him in prayer.

Vigorous singing followed. The songs "came from the depths of their hearts and throbbed with earnestness," Peter noted. "One songbook was shared by five — sometimes ten — people. Most sang from memory."

Three men preached that night in a service that lasted for three hours. The closing speaker took his text from Romans 10:13, "Whoever calls on the name of the Lord shall be saved."

While the service was in progress, Peter noticed several uniformed Russian soldiers standing in the congregation. They were listening with great interest, convincing Peter that the Gospel had not lost its power in a land which had officially declared itself atheistic. During a time of prayer at the close of the service, Peter noticed that even those soldiers bowed their heads in reverence as sinners cried out to God for mercy. He wrote home that he was "thoroughly convinced that people in Russia are hungry for the Gospel of Jesus Christ."

When the service ended, a couple came forward to be united in marriage. They had been sitting on one of the few seats during the service and stepped forward as the preacher announced, "Sey-chas budyem eemet brakosochetanie [We will now proceed with the marriage]."

The entire congregation strained to see as the young bride and groom knelt before the minister. The couple stood as the pastor admonished them to live a holy married life. The choir sang several hymns suitable for the occasion, including *God, Give Them Happiness* and *Two Hands Before God*. They knelt and prayed again until the pastor pronounced the benediction and invited the gathered friends to greet the young couple.

Some of the churches Peter visited in Kiev — including Baptist, Evangelical, Lutheran, and Russian Orthodox — had as many as four services each week. They met in simple, unadorned halls because the ornate Greek Orthodox monasteries had been closed since 1930. No longer could the faithful make their pilgrimages, when they sometimes walked thousands of miles to say their prayers under the gold-plated domes. The great churches of old were now used as antireligion museums, where students and tourists were shown the relics of various religions which had flourished in their country before communism was introduced.

During his visit to one of these museums in Kiev, Peter was guided through many underground tunnels where he saw collections of sacred objects which had been kept by the monks and worshiped by the weary pilgrims. Peter took his tour on Monday, the Russian day of rest at that time. Clusters of children, out of school for the day, mingled with him on the tour. They heard lectures in which God and religion were criticized and impudently denigrated, reminding Peter once again of the dark shadow that gripped his homeland.

✦•✦ ═◆═ •✦•

An early-morning express train on Tuesday took Peter overnight to Moscow. His Intourist guide failed to meet his train at 11:00 a.m., leaving him puzzled concerning his next move. An hour passed before he could determine where he should go and what he should do. Finally, the communist chief of the station called a taxi and worked out the details of his Moscow visit.

"It pays to travel with God!" Peter wrote. "Jesus is the best Friend you can have in this world."

This same truth carried him to St. Petersburg and across the Soviet Union on the trans-Siberian express train bound for Otpor and the Manchurian border. He continued on to Tientsin and Shanghai in China, and then on to Japan.

The Japanese gave Peter some trying moments following his arrival to speak at a meeting of Russian believers in Tokyo. The phone rang in his room at approximately 5:00 p.m. A man speaking English was calling from the front desk.

"Mr. Deyneka?"

"Yes."

"You are required to appear at police headquarters at 10:00 tomorrow morning. They want to talk to you."

"Police?" Peter asked, astonished. "What do they want?"

"Well," the voice said, "I don't know, but you must go there."

"How do they even know I'm here?" Peter asked. "I just arrived!"

"I don't know," the voice replied.

"But I am an American citizen. Do they want to see my passport?"

"No, they want to see you!"

Peter began pacing the room. *After traveling all through Europe, Siberia, and China without any trouble,* he thought, *now here in Tokyo the police want to arrest me!* Instead of sleeping that night, he spent the hours praying hard for the Lord's protection.

The following morning, Peter took a taxi to the police headquarters. The chief questioned Peter extensively on where he had been and why he had come to Japan, writing down each answer in detail. For three and a half hours the evangelist answered pointed questions, not knowing the reason for the grilling.

"How did you know I was in Tokyo?" Peter finally asked.

The policeman explained that a pastor at one of the churches in which Peter had arranged to speak had informed the police that a Russian-born visitor would be in his pulpit. "We will be in that church to hear you," the police chief promised.

Afterward, several officers took Peter to a café where they bought him some tea and continued to ask numerous questions until they were satisfied with his report.

As had been the case in dozens of other cities, Peter's sermons were accompanied by strong conviction which fell upon his audience. The pastor asked the people to remain after the service and pray. Most of them did, bursting forth in spontaneous praise and prayer.

As Peter left the service on the last evening he was there, a policeman met him at a side door. "I have something for you, Rev. Deyneka," he said, holding out a large, beautiful bouquet of flowers. "Please accept these as a token from the police force of Tokyo. We sincerely hope that you will come again."

Peter carried the flowers with him on the train to Yokohama where he boarded a ship bound for Seattle, reserving the last berth on the small vessel. He left just a few days before war broke out between China and Japan. He had circled the world and found Russians in every single city he visited. He didn't know it then, but SGA-sponsored missionaries would eventually follow him to those fields and beyond.

The following year Peter established work among Russian-Aleuts. The Russians had discovered and populated Alaska's Aleutian Islands in the mid-1700s. Peter found people with names like Stepanoff and Osbekoff. Their ancestors had intermarried years before with Russian fur traders and had begun following Russian customs. These Russian-speaking Aleuts had a knowledge of church ritualism, but few had heard of the Gospel of Jesus Christ.

In the spring of 1939, SGA's first North American missionary, Walter Covich, heard the challenge of missions in the northland and established a witness among these Russian-speaking Aleuts. This ministry grew to sponsor 20 missionaries in eight locations working in one of the world's most remote areas.

That same year Peter Deyneka traveled to Cuba, and in 1940 to the continent of South America which openly embraced SGA's ministries to Russians. SGA was on the move — a rapidly expanding mission to a rapidly expanding mission field.

9

SOUTH TO THE HARVEST

In 1940, more than two years after circling the globe with one message about one faith for one world, Peter Deyneka turned his attention to Russians living on the fourth largest continent — South America. Nearly twice the size of the United States, it offered the eager Russian evangelist "twice the blessing."

SGA workers prepared for Peter's trip by praying specifically that if he were to begin a ministry to Russians living in Latin America, enough gifts designated for such a trip would be contributed. By November 1949, his round-trip ticket was purchased and a farewell meeting took place at the Russian Evangelical Christian Church of Chicago.

Peter sailed from New York on the *S.S. Brazil* with his Bible in hand and a heart full of faith. On the first Sunday at sea, the ship's captain asked him to conduct services in the first-class section for all passengers aboard. "I couldn't refuse," Peter admitted. "I had promised the Lord I would be ready anytime and anywhere — even on the sea — to witness for Him." After the service, the captain asked the enthusiastic Russian preacher to lead the remaining two services of the voyage.

Seventeen days after leaving New York, the ship docked at Rio de Janeiro where Peter boarded a train for Sao Paulo to meet his first fellow Russian believers in South America.

A Russian brother took him 300 miles inland to visit Russian colonies in Uruguay. The land the Europeans farmed could only be rented for seven years in one place. Consequently, he found his people living in mud houses with tin roofs. When the seven years were up, they destroyed their homes, took the tin roofs with them, and moved to another place to remain for another seven years. Peter's meetings were held in temporary homes like these.

"People here are hungry for the Word of God," Peter wrote home. "There is immediate need for a trained Russian Christian worker here. Please pray!"

At a train station farther into Uruguay, Peter was met by the leader of an evangelical Christian church and three other brethren. He arrived at the beginning of harvest. By horse and wagon he rumbled over dirt roads through fields of golden wheat, eventually arriving at the humble home of his Russian host. Inside, a group of neighbors had already gathered and eagerly welcomed Peter to their farming community.

Word of a visiting Russian "kinsman" traveled fast, and quickly the lane was dotted with Russians on foot and in wagons, making their way to the house gathering where Peter opened his Russian-language Bible to expound to hungry hearts its life-giving message. His travel diary records the results: "Hearts were melted, believers revived, backsliders reclaimed, sinners converted. Thank God for this great hunger for the Bread of Life."

In just a few days, the farmers became Peter's friends. He found it difficult to break away when the time came to depart for Argentina. "The love of Christ has bound us together," he told the Russian settlers.

A contingent of them left the harvest to accompany him to the train station in Paysandu to send him on his missionary journey southward. Many wept. "We had waited for such a long time for your coming," they told him. "Now you must leave so soon?"

As Peter surveyed the crowd of humble Russian peasant farmers, he could not assume that they would ever meet again on this earth. But he determined in his heart that he would continue his fellowship with them through the universal bond of prayer.

A train took Peter to the eastern coast where he boarded a ship for Buenos Aires. As he stepped from the gangplank of that ship, Peter quickly realized there would be difficulties in his preaching mission to Argentina.

"You are to come with us, Brother Deyneka!" a group of believers called out to him.

"No!" another group insisted. "You must come with us!"

Peter was unable to determine who were his true hosts. "Please, let me first get my baggage," he said, holding up his hands for quiet. "I will try to visit you all."

Peter checked his notebook and sought out the party with whom he had corresponded about the meetings. It was agreed that he would go with him and his party first, then preach to the other group later.

"Many who came from Europe 10 or 12 years ago have fallen into a backslidden condition," Peter wrote home. "There is no one to lead them. I have found coldness and bitterness. But, thank God, there were a few who had faithfully been praying for many years that a spiritual revival would visit their people."

The missionary discovered that some of these people now living in Argentina he had met while they were still in Poland. To several he had given New Testaments which they still carried with them.

In the evenings, Peter preached in scheduled services. During the days, he met a stream of discouraged and defeated people hoping to find deliverance from their problems. Sometimes he counseled with people from 9:00 a.m. until well into the night.

One particular service boldly stands out in Peter's South American experiences — a service at a Baptist church in Buenos Aires where the Russians held their meetings each Lord's Day. The memorable service began shortly after supper and lasted until midnight.

"What crying out to God!" Peter wrote. "The people confessed sins to one another, praised God for the Holy Spirit, and rejoiced in the spiritual renewal which had swept through their church."

Nobody wanted to go home. People embraced each other, sometimes with tears, as they asked forgiveness for hard feelings. Then they prayed some more, giving thanks to God. "I cannot describe to you what took place in that meeting." Peter said.

As they were on their knees praising God, two brethren whispered to Peter that they must go to another community where there were Russian families who needed God. These men left immediately and reached their destination at 1:00 a.m. As they entered the first house they shouted, "Everybody get up! God is working in the church. Great miracles have happened. Get up! Get right with God and with each other."

A lady of the house at once got out of bed and began to weep and pray to God. Then the visitors went to another house, calling on their friends to rouse themselves from sleep in order to enjoy the revival that God had brought to their stale, tired, and troubled assembly. In a third house three families gathered in one room for prayer, repenting and asking God not to pass them by.

"We did not sleep all night," the brethren said to Peter in the morning, after they had returned from their journey. "We spent all our time praying for the Russian people of South America."

The stress and strain of travel, all-day counseling, and extensive preaching drained Peter of physical strength. But in the midst of it all he testified that "my heart is overflowing with joy." Each time he looked into a Russian face, he felt an overpowering urge to ensure that person had made peace with God.

One of those faces belonged to a man in obvious misery. The Russian had migrated to South America 11 years earlier, leaving his wife and son. In the New World he had fallen into sin, forgetting his family. When Peter was in Russia in 1937, he had met the wife of this man. She had begged him to help find her husband in South America, and now here in a Gospel service Peter was preaching to him.

Part of the way through the sermon, the man sent a note to the preacher asking Peter to pray for him immediately. The note also asked the entire congregation to unite in prayer for him. "I let the man struggle a while longer under his conviction," Peter stated. "I felt he needed the extra time to let God speak to him."

During the rest of Peter's message, the man wept constantly. When Peter closed the meeting with an invitation for Christians to surrender their lives to God, people started to stream toward the altar. Some almost ran. Many were in tears. The presence of the Lord filled the tiny church where even atheists and strangers had gathered. No one left for two hours.

The man who had left his family in Russia wept as though his heart had broken under the weight of conviction. When the praying subsided, he asked if he could speak to the church. He went to the front of the room, but he was so broken he could not speak for a long while. Finally his story began to spill out. He warned his friends how terrible it is to be a backslider, drifting away from God and living in sin. "Please forgive me," he said. "Please pray for me."

After the service the man came to Peter and explained, "Brother Deyneka, I feel like a new man! A great burden has left my heart. I am so sorry that I wasted my life in sin these past 11 years in South America."

Later the repentant Russian wrote out his testimony and had it printed. "I can boldly testify before all what the Lord has done for me," he wrote. "I can truly say that in my heart I now feel the presence of the Holy Spirit and great joy has filled me. For this, I constantly thank my Lord that He brought me out of the miry clay. Now I can say *Hallelujah!*"

In Buenos Aires, Hebrew missionary Paul Rosenberg invited Peter to speak at his Hebrew Christian Mission — the only such mission in South America at that time. Peter also addressed a group of Christian businessmen from London, England, preaching in a beautiful new YWCA building to an English-speaking audience. He also spoke at a Spanish Baptist church with an American missionary interpreting.

Another result of the revival in Buenos Aires involved the two different groups who had fought over hosting Peter when he first arrived. Peter discovered during his stay that differences had formed a division between them, but the work of the Holy Spirit mended their ways and healed the rift. As one reunited body, they officially asked Peter to send a trained Gospel worker to lead their united church.

The welcome of Russians in South America was warm and enthusiastic, and the farewells were just as splendid — tearful and full of rejoicing. In Buenos Aires, 37 Russians gathered around singing. Among the group assembled were three Russian communists who had not escaped the finger of God. As Peter climbed aboard the train, he opened the window of the car and offered a prayer just as the train began to move.

"Come back soon and stay longer, Brother Deyneka," they cried out.

The train sped on toward the province of Misiones, Argentina. Peter watched one flat field after another approach and disappear. More than 50,000 Russian and Ukrainian people lived in Misiones. Most of them had come to Argentina a decade earlier. They had found only a few Indians living on the territory. With the free land given them by the Argentine government, the Russian farmers felled the timber and fought to clear the land for crops. But before the land began to produce, the pioneers endured great poverty.

Roads had been cut through the fields of red clay, but the least amount of rain turned them into unpassable sloughs of mud. On one trip, as Peter bounced along on a 12-mile journey by horse and wagon, he often had to get out and help the horse pull the wagon through the ruts. But the roads dried quickly with a small amount of sunshine, bringing to vivid color the beautiful orchards of banana, orange, and lemon trees.

In Misiones, heat and humidity plagued Peter, but the revival meetings went on. Even though summer fruits and grain had to be harvested, the people made time to come hear the evangelist. Many people walked to the services, coming from all parts of the province. A spirit of repentance and deep searching after God characterized the meetings, just as they always had from the time Peter Deyneka began to preach the Gospel. "When they saw Christians revived," Peter noted, "it was no trouble for the unsaved to come to Christ."

In one service, the moderator announced that Peter would be preaching next in a Gospel mission 25 miles away, yet so many people wanted to attend the meetings that the church had to rent a bus. Still others traveled by horseback, and many walked the day's journey to the chapel.

Peter rode in the bus, arriving hot and tired at 9:00 a.m. to begin the meeting with prayer. "I felt the presence of God as soon as I began to speak," he said. "I noticed people weeping. Some even cried out loud, making it difficult for me to continue my message. The revival was on!"

Peter urged the people to obey the Holy Spirit, "whatever the need may be in your life." At once, people fell down on their knees and began to cry out to God.

A lady who had been expelled from the church for backsliding came under deep conviction, seeking the assurance and abiding happiness of her salvation. Another backslider who had been expelled from the church cried out, "Oh God, I am left out. I have lost my fellowship with You and with my brothers and sisters in Christ."

While this prayer was being offered, a man rushed up to Peter from the back of the church. He threw his arms around Peter's neck and cried out, "I want to be saved . . . I want to be saved . . . I want to be saved!" Both men knelt and the convicted man offered the sinner's prayer.

For quite a while the tempest of holy revival continued, sweeping away hard feelings and restoring unity and power to the small congregation of farmers. Peter asked the choir to sing, but they too were under such conviction that they could not finish the selection through their weeping and sobbing.

Peter conducted four meetings that day. At the last evening session, "15 unsaved people rushed to the altar for salvation," while many others throughout the congregation wept. People did not want to return to their farms. Three times Peter told them the meeting was over and begged them to go home, but nobody would move. They wanted to go on.

"Brother," someone cried out, "please tell us some more and let us pray again." The Russians seemed to be prepared to stay all night.

An area-wide revival service was planned for the next morning in the largest church of the district. Three choirs would join to provide the music and the service would be Peter's farewell meeting. Rain had fallen steadily all day and the roads had become more rutted and treacherous.

"We had stayed so long in the church that nobody wanted to go home," Peter reported. "I suggested that before they end the meeting, we all pray and ask God to stop the rain at least until noon the next day if it was His will that we have the farewell gathering."

After the prayer, the rain stopped abruptly. Early the next morning, a hot sun appeared to dry out the roads. Two trucks transported the choir members to the appointed place 25 miles away. The weather remained beautiful until 1:00 p.m. Just as the service ended, dark clouds suddenly hid the sun and rain fell in a cloudburst.

"Brother Deyneka," people chided, "why didn't you pray that there would be no rain all day?" They had to transport their guest through three miles of rain-soaked mud roads to a German Baptist church. When Peter arrived, so many people had gathered that there was no room for the great crowd of latecomers outside.

Again, Peter's preaching was met by stirring revival in which sinners repented of their iniquity, backsliders were reclaimed, and enemies reunited in friendship. The mission to Misiones ended with a baptismal service for new converts, following a side trip to a village where 10,000 Ukrainians had settled.

Paraguay was next on Peter's South American preaching voyage. Here also, thousands of Slavic immigrants had settled. Up the Paraguay River Peter sailed, 25 miles into the back country with a delegation of five Russian brethren from five different provinces. They had come a day early so they wouldn't miss his arrival.

Peter was hot and tired, but he dared not disappoint his hosts. The midsummer heat wilted him quickly, but there was no respite for the visiting preacher. Traveling sometimes on two-wheeled wagons, periodically on foot, and occasionally by horseback, Peter found hungry hearts wherever he went. His hands and ankles were badly bitten by tiny insects and loss of sleep had weakened him, but there was no complaining. "My heart was full of joy and praise to God for the privilege I had to be among these hungry souls," he said.

By train Peter journeyed back to Argentina, arriving in a little town about 6:00 at night. A cluster of Russian and Ukrainian people met him, imploring him to conduct a Gospel meeting. Peter knew there was a congregation gathered in a nearby church awaiting his arrival, so he tried to determine if he should leave immediately or remain to speak to the crowd who had just met him.

After much confusion, he told the brother who had come to escort him that he would not be at the church until the following morning. But instead of leaving to inform the group that Peter would not be coming, the brother remained in the group to hear the visitor's message. Peter had to stop preaching and remind the man to go tell the people.

"Don't worry, Brother Deyneka," he said. "They won't leave until I get there." Peter decided the man's soul was so hungry he wanted to get all he could for himself.

The next day, a four-wheeled wagon drawn by horses took him to a clearing in the woods. It was hot, and Peter hadn't rested very well the night before. As soon as he stepped off the wagon, the leader presented him to the waiting crowd of people: "Here is our brother, for whom we have been waiting."

Peter prayed that God would supply strength. He spoke on the theme *Full Surrender to Christ*. After he had preached for about 30 minutes, the conviction which had characterized his earlier meetings fell on the people. Men, women, and children stood enthralled, listening until Peter's strength and time were gone. He called for prayer and sat down. Earnest Christians among the people began to pray while one man hurried to the platform. "Brother Deyneka," he whispered, "won't you stay longer?"

Peter shook his head. "I'm sorry," he replied, "I must go to other places. If I had my way, I would remain." In his heart, Peter determined to raise up workers in the United States to come and be missionaries to these new friends.

From the rural woodland of Argentina, Peter traveled to Tumoca, Chile, for meetings arranged by workers of the Christian and Missionary

Alliance. Finally he traveled north to Quito, Ecuador, at the invitation of Mr. and Mrs. Clarence Jones, pioneer missionaries who founded Radio Station HCJB. This stopover became historic for Peter. At a casual invitation by Mr. Jones, he preached in the Russian language on history's first Gospel program beamed by shortwave to Russian-speaking people. This broadcast was heard by Mrs. Deyneka in far-off Chicago on a shortwave set. It was to be the first of many thousands of Russian Gospel broadcasts sent out by SGA in cooperation with various missionary radio stations.

Following a brief stop in Havana, Cuba, Peter completed yet another exhaustive international mission trip. After logging thousands of miles, he returned home physically spent but spiritually energized with a strategic plan to recruit workers to help reap the South American harvest.

10

THE SCHOOL THAT PRAYER BUILT

As Peter Deyneka charted his global travels among Slavic peoples, he longed to raise up an army of trained Christian workers to win his countrymen for Jesus Christ. The words of the apostle Paul in Romans 10:14 burned in his heart: "How shall they believe in Him of whom they have not heard? And how shall they hear without a preacher?"

Josef Stalin was busily training workers in atheistic communism, but there was no program of biblical instruction for young Slavic Christians. No Bible-training institution in the world offered pastoral coursework for Russian-speaking young people or served the cultural needs of this segment of youth. Peter knew the time was right to open such a school, but where? How?

In 1943, two years after Peter returned from South America, he met with Pastor Oswald J. Smith of Peoples Church in Toronto. Dr. Smith had made his first visit to Russia in 1924. He went to the borders of Russia again in 1929, and in 1936 he made his third trip. He wrote several magazine articles reporting on his experiences. These stirred the imagination of the Canadian and American public as he wrote of eager Russian listeners, crowded meetings, fervent prayer sessions, and overwhelming responses to the invitation. By the time Peter approached him to discuss the need for a Bible institute to train Russian workers, both the pastor and congregation at Peoples Church were ready for a united effort.

That same year, the first classes of the Russian Bible Institute (RBI) opened in a large room of the educational building at Peoples Church.

Enrollment consisted of 45 students taught by four professors. The program was a three year Bible course covering all the basics such as Bible doctrine, personal evangelism, church history, homiletics, Christian education, pastoral training, missions, hermeneutics, Old and New Testament, and other subjects. All lessons were taught in the Russian language.

In addition, the grammar, vocabulary, and phonetics of the Russian language were taught to help students improve and fortify their use of their mother tongue. For the students who had grown up in a country foreign to their ancestry, Russian literature, culture, and history were other necessary subjects.

In the mid-1940s, following the devastation of World War II, the burgeoning city of Toronto began accommodating a large Slavic population as thousands of refugees and displaced persons poured into Canada from the settlement camps of Germany, Austria, and Czechoslovakia. This brought a new and responsive mission field to RBI's doorstep, providing opportunities for the students to conduct personal evangelism door to door, in the parks, and on the street corners. Most of the immigrants had escaped from Slavic countries where atheism had been taught to them daily. Now at last they were free to hear the Gospel, attend churches, and teach their children about God and the Bible. As a result, children of these refugees began enrolling at RBI to prepare for Christian service.

The unique annual missionary conferences at Peoples Church exposed the students to a global missionary program that was available in few churches in America and Canada. Many responded as Dr. Smith and Rev. Deyneka shared their vision. In seven years, RBI graduated 85 well-trained, dedicated Russian young people. Most were commissioned for full-time Christian service in South America, Korea, Europe, Canada, the Philippines, and the United States.

In February 1944, some SGA missionaries in Argentina formed a committee to seek the best location for a second Russian Bible Institute like the one functioning in Toronto. A large, old building in Rosario, Argentina, was selected as the facility in which to launch the project, but God would need to raise up teachers and other needed personnel.

Young people from Russian churches in Chicago were challenged by Peter to enlist their services for missions. Some were trained at Moody Bible Institute and went on to work in Alaska, Europe, Australia, and South America. The earliest workers at the new school in Argentina were among these recruited from Peter's home city.

Two of the Slavic young people from the Chicago team were Constantine Lewshenia and Mary Beechick. Mary was first to respond to the call for workers in Argentina. About a year later, Const also left for South America, together with Sam Fewchuk, a Ukrainian from Canada whose life had been influenced by Peter Deyneka.

"Why don't you stop at HCJB in Quito and give a hand with the Russian radio broadcasts?" Peter suggested. So Const's first assignment was at a microphone addressing millions of fellow Slavs in Europe and the Americas. Sam went on to Argentina where he did two things — he married Mary Beechick, whom he had met in Chicago, and became one of the founders of RBI in Rosario.

A fourth member of the Chicago team, Russian-born Elizabeth Zernov, heard God's call to South America. Elizabeth, with four sisters, two brothers, and their parents, had come from Russia in 1929 to settle in Beaver Dam, Wisconsin. Peter Deyneka's abundant enthusiasm and vision reached that home. In time, four of the talented Zernov daughters became workers and missionaries with SGA.

Elizabeth's first assignment was in Quito to help establish the Russian department of the global broadcasts aired daily by Radio Station HCJB. She came by plane — unlike Const, Sam, and Mary, who had taken the long way to the mission field, enduring lengthy boat travel and arduous train trips through the Andes Mountains. Const and Elizabeth became better acquainted in Quito and fell in love. By the time Const left for Argentina, they were engaged.

As the end of March 1944 approached and the time to officially open the new school neared, concern arose as to whether or not there would be enough students. Only a few applications were in hand. Yet a few days before opening on April 1, more students began to arrive. Many brought their application forms with them instead of mailing them. Others came with friends who had not even bothered to fill out the application forms. A total of 26 students enrolled that first year.

In 1945, Rev. Moses Gitlin, a prominent Russian Hebrew-Christian, arrived from RBI in Toronto to assist in teaching and preparing curriculum at the newly established school in Argentina. Since Gitlin came via Quito, Elizabeth Zernov joined him for the journey to Argentina where her fiancé Const had been patiently waiting for 22 months. Thirteen days after they arrived in Argentina, Professor Gitlin united Const and Elizabeth in holy matrimony.

During vacations and holidays, the student body scattered to the backwoods of Argentina to put into practical use the lessons they had learned. The faculty joined them as the Fewchuks, Lewshenias, and Professor Gitlin traveled throughout Uruguay, Paraguay, Argentina, and into Brazil to minister to Slavic colonies. They also recruited students for RBI.

Because the Slavic community in South America remained a small minority, the student body was never large, but each student was seriously committed to missionary work. An average of 85 percent of each class stepped out into active Christian service.

In 1949, Const and Elizabeth Lewshenia returned to Radio Station HCJB. Sam and Mary Fewchuk went to pioneer areas of Australia. But God raised up new teachers and workers as RBI expanded its influence among new and larger Slavic communities. Under God's blessing, the institute prospered. When the school in Toronto was discontinued in 1950, the school in Argentina became the world's only Russian Bible Institute.

In 1956 — the year RBI moved from Rosario to Buenos Aires — Andrew and Pauline Semenchuk arrived. Andrew was born in Russia, but came to Canada with his parents at the age of four. Peter Deyneka's frequent visits to the little country church that the Semenchuks attended made a lasting impression on the young man. Andrew was among the first to eagerly enroll in the first class of RBI in Toronto.

Meanwhile, Peter Deyneka's influence reached another Slavic home in Chicago to touch the life of Pauline Mazur. This daughter of a Russian Orthodox priest had a godly mother who eventually won her husband to the Lord Jesus Christ. Pauline was also enrolled at RBI in Toronto where she met Andrew. After graduation and marriage, they returned to Chicago where Andrew finished seminary training and prepared himself for ministries in Europe, Alaska, and South America. Andrew directed the Argentina school for 12 years, launching evening sessions and special classes to train lay leaders of the Russian evangelical churches in Buenos Aires in addition to the regular curriculum.

The yearbooks of the Russian Bible Institutes are filled with an honor roll of stalwart Slavic pioneer missionaries. Jack Koziol was born in the Ukraine and raised in Canada. Upon graduation from RBI, he and his wife, Vera, began their ministry among Slavic immigrants in Canada. Later they directed Slavic ministries to Russia at Radio Station HLKX in South Korea, as well as prepared and produced many programs at Far East Broadcasting Company's complex in the Philippines.

Alex Kuvshinikov was born in Russia and became a Christian in Pennsylvania. He enrolled at RBI in Argentina where he met Elodia, a Russian from Paraguay who became his wife. Their mission field to Slavic people was first in Seoul at HLKX. Alex sent the message of Jesus Christ into the region of Siberia — the very area where his uncle was once imprisoned under Josef Stalin for the Gospel's sake. The Kuvshinikovs later continued their Russian radio ministry at HCJB.

Basilio Polischuk entered RBI to learn how to witness more effectively among forgotten Russians living in a Spanish culture and working in meat-packing factories, drinking themselves into blurred forgetfulness. Basilio and his family eventually went to live among those disadvantaged Russians, distributing God's Word, pointing young and old to joy and happiness through faith in Jesus Christ.

Other graduates from RBI are Mary and Nicholas Slobodian. These devoted missionaries have preached to Argentine Russians from the sun-baked cotton fields to the bustling cities. They have experienced many adventures throughout the course of their ministry, as was the case when they met the drunken husband of a faithful Russian parishioner.

"If you baptize my wife, I'll kill her and you too!" he raged against Mary and Nicholas.

For several months the Slobodians had driven every week through the hot fields to visit Russian families living in remote Slavic colonies. In one sad home they had met this woman and her alcoholic husband. At first the husband was intrigued by the Bible's message of hope which he had never heard before. Then his son, daughter-in-law, and their 11 children who lived on a nearby farm all came to hear Nicholas preach.

Their son's family was also in great need. Like his father, the son was an alcoholic. His large family lived in a bedraggled, two-room, adobe shelter and barely subsisted on a few acres of neglected land. But as the Slobodians continued to visit, the son came to the Lord and was cleansed of sin and his tragic habit.

Gradually the entire family came to the Lord — except the father. He continued to rage at his Christian wife and repeatedly beat her. Many nights she slept in the woods to escape his wrath. Despite her husband's threats, she insisted that she must be baptized. "Even if I only live a day or two, I want to be baptized," she told her husband.

Reluctantly, the Slobodians finally agreed to baptize the determined new convert, her son, daughter-in-law, and their 11 children. Aware of the danger from the father, the new converts and the Slobodians prepared for the baptism. The father also made preparations to carry out his threats.

The day of the baptisms came. Stayed by the hand of the Lord, and perhaps convicted by the sight of so many of his family following the Lord, the father hung at the edge of the crowd that had gathered for the baptism. He did no harm as his family entered the water.

"Who would have cared for this outcast Russian family if we hadn't?" the Slobodians ask. "We had to. They were *naschi* — some of our own Russian people."

And *naschi* continue to enroll in the only Russian Bible institute in the world. It's the school that prayer built, and it still functions today by that same spiritual discipline.

11

NEW FRUIT IN NEW ORCHARDS

The misery of World War II lingered on in the wretched European camps that had been designed for displaced persons (DPs) — people spun off from the horror of the conflict. These crowded cauldrons of human misery became homes for thousands of Slavic refugees who had been thrust out of their countries or who refused to return to Russia after the war. Year after year they waited in congested camps in Germany and Austria, hoping for resettlement and a new life in a free country. Among the two million DPs were souls for whom Christ died, and Peter Deyneka launched a Gospel offensive to reach them.

SGA's headquarters became a depot for processing hundreds of food and clothing packages earmarked for Slavic DPs. With the relief parcels went missionaries to offer the Bread of Life as well.

For the rest of the 1940s and into the 1950s, Peter regularly traveled to the DP camps in many parts of Europe. Hearts there were open to receive the Good News, and sometimes he would remain there for several months. Young Slavic workers from North America joined Peter for the combined work of relief and evangelism to a captive mission field ripe for Kingdom harvests.

The recruitment of young evangelists for the camps was an effective strategy of drawing many new missionaries into lifetime service with the mission. What the young people saw, they could never forget. The meetings generated a new compassion for their own people and fired their zeal to be Christ's hands and feet and voice among them.

One of the first recruits was Ruth Deyneka, eldest child of Peter and Vera. After transferring from RBI in Toronto and graduating from Bob Jones University, Ruth accompanied her father to Europe to work in the refugee camps for the summer. But at the end of the 90-day stint, Ruth did not want to leave. Her heart had been broken by the desperate needs of the people and their tragic stories.

On the day she was to sail home with her father, she made her decision to remain. She went to Southampton, England, with her father and helped him unpack in his stateroom aboard the *R.M.S. Queen Mary* that would carry him to the United States.

"Are you sure you want to stay in Europe, Ruthie?" Peter asked.

"Yes, Papa, I'm sure."

"Do you need some money?"

Ruth shook her head. "Why do I need money? I have $10 in my pocketbook, friends back in the United States who care about my ministry, and my ticket to get back to the refugee camp in Germany. If Mama sends me CARE packages, I'll be all right."

Peter wept as he hugged his daughter and said goodbye. They knelt together and prayed, committing each other to the Lord. "Her courage touched my heart," he said later.

Back in the DP camps Ruth was joined by Roza Kucher, a girl of Russian heritage from a Slavic community in western Canada. For a year and a half they ministered together, sang hymns, and played their instruments.

Roza vividly recalls one incident when she and Ruth were conducting a meeting in a German camp. "I stood on the platform — one young, rather tremulous girl, facing rows of sad, haggard, Slavic people. I had just finished speaking from the Bible and praying. I asked all who wanted to accept Christ as Savior to stand. In response, the *entire* audience rose. I began to weep at the evident spiritual hunger, feeling helpless to counsel so many. I had studied personal evangelism as a student at the Toronto Russian Bible Institute, but I never expected anything like this.

"My co-laborer, Ruth, was also choked with emotion, 'Pray, Roz,' she whispered, 'Pray! Tell the people to repeat the prayer after you.' And as I prayed each phrase, a roar of response resounded from the audience. Hearts were eagerly opened to receive the Lord."

Both Roza and Ruth met their future husbands in Europe. In 1951 Nick Leonovich, a Russian relative of the Deynekas from New Jersey, felt God's call to work among the DPs. In Europe he met and married Roza, where they continued their ministries under SGA's sponsorship. In 1958, they initiated Russian-language Gospel broadcasts at Trans World Radio which Paul Freed founded in Tangier, Morocco. Later, Nick and Roza continued this radio ministry to Russian-speaking people from Monte Carlo, Monaco. Over the years, Gospel broadcasts beamed from the TWR transmitters brought bountiful blessings to the former Soviet Union.

In a DP camp at Trieste, Italy, Ruth was reintroduced to Jack Shalanko whom she had first met when they both attended the Toronto Russian Bible Institute. After their marriage in 1953, they went to South America where they established a fruitful ministry at the microphones of Radio Station HCJB in Quito, Ecuador, ministering to Russian people around the world.

Other missionaries emerged from among the ranks of the DPs. Agripina Bardanova had been a wealthy woman in Russia before World War I. In the early 1900s, she had made a profitable living smuggling goods from the region of Siberia to western Russia. In 1929, she married and moved with her husband to Latvia. As the bride of a successful businessman, she had all the material comforts and social prestige anyone could want. She had three homes and money to travel, yet she was unhappy — restless and searching.

In 1929, Agripina heard Dr. Oswald J. Smith from Toronto when he visited Riga, Latvia. She opened her heart in that service and experienced the transforming power of Jesus Christ. She began at once to witness of her faith to others. Just as she had conducted the affairs of her prior business life, she worked equally as fervently for her new Master.

Ten years later, World War II drove Agripina and her husband to Italy where her husband died. Agripina was left penniless. SGA missionaries found her in Rome and assisted Agripina in her dire poverty. The widow heard Peter Deyneka preach and determined she would spend the rest of her life witnessing among her own people. She used to say, "I will never retire from serving Christ. I'll only stop when the Lord takes me home." And she did, energetically carrying out a witness among Slavic immigrants and Italians in Rome, distributing tens of thousands of Gospel tracts.

━━┥ ⋈✦⋈ ┝━━

During the years that Peter Deyneka was circling the globe, establishing new missionary outreaches and ministering to Russians, he also tirelessly cultivated supporters in North America. Hardly any evangelical Christian was without some knowledge of the man who was "rushing the Gospel to the Russians." His "home" for a good portion of the time was a hotel room, a train depot, or an airport. "I felt like I knew the inside of every train and plane," he said.

Peter's broken English and short-clipped syntax, laced with a heavy Russian accent, could have impeded his speaking presentation. But instead he turned it to his advantage with thundering sermons and strong appeals, confirming his well-earned nickname of Peter Dynamite. People who heard his powerful messages often commented, "He carries his own loudspeaker with him wherever he goes." From big auditoriums to tiny churches he went, calling for helpers to assist him in bringing the Gospel to Slavic peoples.

One of the smaller congregations was Farmerstown Mennonite Church in Ohio with a tiny missionary budget. Pastor Homer Kandel had become concerned about the church's ignorance of missions. He had read Peter's book *Much Prayer — Much Power*, along with books by Oswald Smith, and they had greatly influenced him and his people to become more active in missionary support.

The first year, with just 80 members, the Farmerstown Mennonites pledged the astonishing amount of $16,000. The second year the offerings increased to $25,000 and the third year totalled $35,000. In the fourth year, with a church membership increase of only 12 people, the pledge figure was $45,000. As the years went by, the offerings reached as high as $100,00 per year, and the fervor spread to other churches.

In the early 1940s, SGA was able to open branch offices in England, Australia, New Zealand, and South America to serve believers outside North America whose hearts God had touched by appeals to help. The list of men supporting Peter's ministry grew larger with the spread of the mission's scope — Torrey Johnson, Roy Strobeck, Bob Swanson, Robert Kinney, Eugene Johnson, Warren Wiersbe, Charles Bodeen, Bob Cook, Evon Hedley, Jack Wyrtzen, Billy Graham, Charles E. Fuller, George Sweeting, Robert Bowman, Stephen Olford, and many others.

Although unlettered in the deeper tenets of theology and unlearned in school-taught methods of evangelism, Peter almost always enjoyed spiritual power in his sermons and fruit for his labors. His message was simple, as were his tastes for material blessings. A loaf of black bread and some salami from his briefcase were all he needed for a satisfying meal.

Once in England, following World War II, Billy Graham was conducting evangelistic services in the Liverpool City auditorium while Peter was there speaking at SGA meetings. Old friends from years gone by, the two men met and prayed together for God's blessings throughout their time in England, and then went to dine with Cliff and Billie Barrows. In the wake of the war, rations at the restaurant were scarce and very little bread was available. Peter pulled a tube of salami and dark bread carefully wrapped in newspaper from his ubiquitous briefcase. Billie Barrows had some butter from a rationing coupon, so bread was distributed and meat provided to the grateful participants as they enjoyed their humble meal.

In mass meetings or with individuals, Peter was ready at any moment to talk about his Lord. On a trip to Australia in the 1960s, he had a four-hour layover. A stewardess asked him, "And what business are you in?"

"I'm a preacher of the Gospel," Peter replied.

"What is the Gospel?" asked the puzzled woman. She had just a few minutes left to visit, but Peter quickly shared with her from the Bible how the hope of the Gospel is for all people.

"That's strange," the woman replied. "I've been going to church for 17 years and I've never even heard the word 'Gospel' in our church." She asked several more questions, then turned to leave.

"Would you like to know Christ as your personal Savior?" Peter asked.

"Yes," the stewardess replied softly.

Peter prayed with her and promised to send her a New Testament and his book *Much Prayer — Much Power*.

Several weeks later, Peter was again passing through Sydney en route to the Philippines when the same stewardess approached him. Peter was overjoyed to see her smile and hear her say, "Do you remember me? I received your literature and read your book. I'm following the Lord now."

These types of stories followed Peter wherever he went. In home-town Chicago, SGA conducted meetings in various parts of the city in addition to broadcasting a weekly, Russian-language Gospel radio show. Basil, a Russian immigrant, was a drug addict. He came to one of the meetings in Chicago, spoke of his addiction to drugs, and expressed his opinion that his case was hopeless. But Peter urged him not to give up. "Please keep coming to our meetings," he implored. "You will hear the truth that can set you free. I am praying for you."

The desperate boy was so lonely to hear the Russian language spoken that he returned again and again, and each time the message of the

Gospel penetrated deeper. Basil was eventually converted and went on to attend Bible school, eventually becoming a pastor in the eastern United States. Persistence and faithful witnessing led a bashful Russian peasant boy to become a bold proclaimer of the Gospel.

Over more than half a century of preaching, the number of "Basils" influenced by Peter Deyneka is hard to tally. Because one lonely immigrant from the Old World found new life at Moody Church in Chicago, many thousands have found the eternal bliss of heaven.

12

NO ROOF
OVER RUSSIA

At the red flash of the "ON THE AIR" light, Peter leaned forward in his chair and began: "Dorogeeye Radio-slushatelyee." In less than a second, those words were flung across the ocean from HCJB in Ecuador to Chomsk, Kiev, Moscow, and the Siberian plains.

It was March 1941. The new tool of evangelistic radio among Slavic people had begun its strategic endeavor. The message with which Peter Deyneka initiated Gospel broadcasts for Slavic people was picked up in Chicago by his wife on a shortwave receiver. She sent a cable which read: "Glad to hear your voice and message — came in very clear."

Bibles are the most significant way to feed the spiritually hungry, but back then they were usually allowed no farther than the Soviet border. Despite all the creative and persistent ways that were attempted to get Bibles beyond the border, the trickle getting through did not begin to meet the demands of 250 million people. But the expanse of radio could reach the ears of eager listeners.

Peter delivered 16 sermons over Radio Station HCJB in those first broadcasts, then returned home to Chicago to closely monitor the response. He quickly became convinced that this vast and fruitful medium for the Gospel could be successfully utilized to reach beyond the Iron Curtain, so he hurriedly set out to enlist other radio preachers to help continue the effort.

Other mission agencies would eventually follow Peter's pioneering efforts until as many as 1,000 Russian-language Gospel broadcasts were flooding his native land each month, beamed from the crackling transmitters of ten international radio stations. The 600 monthly broadcasts produced by SGA alone reached more people than the apostle Paul addressed throughout his entire lifetime.

Because their own internal stations utilize the shortwave medium, Russians traditionally invest heavily in shortwave receivers. Thus, they are large and powerful enough to receive broadcasts from Christian stations in Korea, Western Europe, South America, the Philippines, and the United States. With an estimated 40 million shortwave receivers in use within the Soviet Union at that time, this offered unparalleled opportunities to share the Gospel with millions sequestered in atheistic countries. Peter and his staff knew that their unseen congregation was a large one.

One listener shared this burst of enthusiasm for radio evangelism: "If you were to preach to a crowd of 10,000 people, that would only be 10,000. But when you preach over the radio, hundreds of thousands — even millions — listen to you! Many are buying radios for the first time for the sole purpose of listening to you. Those who do not have enough money pool their funds with others to buy a radio. When you pray, thousands of people all across the Soviet Union are joining you in prayer."

Radio was often the main source of Christian information for Russian believers, so missionaries would prepare special programs to instruct lay preachers. They would also read the Bible at dictation speed so that listeners could write down portions of Scripture and have part of the Bible for their very own. In fact, some listeners would write and say, "Do continue to read the Scriptures on your radio programs, but please slow down. We cannot write that fast!"

Since there were no Bible schools or seminaries for evangelical Christians anywhere in Russia at that time, SGA also broadcast *Bible Institute of the Air*. This program featured daily Bible studies and exposition of the Word, systematically progressing through Scripture for the benefit of pastors and church leaders who depended upon this source for their weekly sermons. Other specialized programs were broadcast for Russian children who had no Sunday schools. Many listeners would write to say that the radio programs were their only church.

Radio also provided open doors for Slavic missionaries who traveled in Eastern Europe. One such pastor took a train to meet citizens of a small village in northern Poland who were regular listeners to the Gospel programs. He had planned on his first visit just to meet the six listeners who had written to request Bibles. But by the time he arrived at the fourth house, such a large group of children were following him that he sat down and began telling them stories from the Bible. He also taught them to sing Gospel hymns.

Suddenly a young Polish man excitedly rushed up to the pastor and announced, "Sir, you must come to my house now and have a meeting. We are all waiting for you. Believers from all over the village have come together to hear you preach."

As the pastor approached the house, he was amazed to see it jammed with people. Some were standing outside the door; others were looking in through the windows. Inside the house, he noticed a statue of Mary and two candles displayed on a table at one end of the parlor. He had anticipated a Protestant meeting, forgetting that most of the people in the countryside were Roman Catholic.

"May the name of Jesus Christ be blessed," the pastor exclaimed as he entered the room.

"And forever and ever may it be blessed," all the people responded.

Villagers who had been discouraged by their church to read the Bible were noticeably excited when the visiting speaker opened his copy of God's Word and began to speak. No one moved for an hour as he expounded about the grace of God and the love of the Savior for the lost.

When he had finished speaking, the pastor suggested he teach them a song about God's love. As if they were children, they eagerly memorized each phrase.

For three hours, the villagers remained squeezed into the small room, singing and listening as the visiting missionary talked to them about the Lord. Eventually becoming fearful that such a meeting might arouse suspicion or antagonism on the part of the local authorities, he told them he must leave.

"I have copies of God's Book here if you want one for yourself," he said, holding a New Testament above his head. The people pressed forward to receive a copy.

"Wait!" a farmer exclaimed. He took his hat, shook it out, and passed it around. "Let us show our gratitude by helping to pay for the Bibles," he said as he took up an offering of thanks.

Finally, the crowd moved away. One old man remained behind, telling the pastor, "I must show you something." He brought out a large, old New Testament — so old that many pages were soiled and crumbling.

"My father was in the Russian navy during the Russo-Japanese War of 1905 in Korea," he said. "An American missionary there gave him this Bible. When my father died, he left it to me. All these years I have waited for someone to come and explain this book. And today, the Lord answered my prayer."

The hunger of these villagers for spiritual food was typical of millions in areas served by broadcasts in Slavic languages. Excerpts from the steady flow of letters sent by listeners reveal hearts that were seeking to make peace with the Creator . . .

> What a joy it is to listen to your broadcasts! There is no greater thrill for me than to have fellowship with His children. I am so thankful to God for this opportunity.
>
> — a postcard from Ukraine

> If it is possible, please send us the words to at least two or three of your songs so that when you sing these hymns, we can join in your beautiful singing.
>
> We don't have a Bible and we don't have fellowship with other Christians because there are no Christians nearby. All we can do is pray and continue to listen to your programs.
>
> — a listener in Ukraine

> Some dear friends of ours frequently listened to HCJB, and Jack Shalanko's messages always gripped them. As a result, the man accepted the Lord. He soon became ill and endured great suffering in the hospital. As his wife sat beside his bed, he lifted his hand to summon her. When she asked what he wanted he murmured, "I want to hear Brother Shalanko preach." They tried to tune in the radio, but shortly after that the man was taken home.
>
> Just before he died, his wife asked him, "What heritage are you leaving us?" He answered with the words of a hymn, "Christ's precious blood and righteousness."
>
> — from Kazakhstan

> I have been listening to your broadcasts regularly for four years now. I know there are many Christians and others lis-

tening to your programs. In this vast desert land, your programs are a wellspring of refreshment for the weary.

— a student from the region of Siberia

I am 23 years old and have completed nine years of education. I work in a factory as a lathe operator. I spend most of my spare time by the radio listening to musical programs on foreign stations. This is how I accidentally discovered your programs. Personally, I don't consider myself a believer or an unbeliever. I've never attended any religious gathering in this city, and I don't even know if any exist. But no matter what anyone says, I am interested in listening to your programs.

— from Kuybishev, Russia

I was young and in love, but the girl I wanted to marry spurned my proposal. Enraged, I tried to kill her. She recovered, but I was sentenced to ten years in a Russian prison.

I came across your Christian programs on my radio here at the prison, and they have made a positive impression on my miserable soul. Now, I cannot live even one day without listening to your broadcasts. I want to follow Christ, but can the Lord forgive a sin so great as mine?

— Dimitri Alexeyevich

Not every writer is sympathetic to the Gospel messages preached on the broadcasts . . .

I often listen to your broadcasts and for a long time have wanted to write to you. I do not know if this will reach you, but I decided to try.

I don't believe your programs are dangerous — you do not mention politics — and for the most part I like the singing and music. I always enjoy music, regardless of who transmits it. And even though I may not understand the words, the music always has a pleasing effect on me. But this is not the reason I write to you.

In your broadcasts you convincingly ask listeners to pray to God and ask Him for mercy, that He would forgive us of our sins. About what kind of sins are you speaking? Can it really be that we have so many of them that we should ask for mercy and, as you say, a miracle will happen? Here in the Soviet Union, people believed that nonsense 50 years ago. But God didn't help them very much.

The question that is of great interest to me is this: Do you truly believe in God? Do you believe sincerely or is it because of your wages? It seems that your God is very friendly with the wealthy and powerful. Very likely you do not live by miracles but by some kind of financial means.

There has not been such a miracle that a man living in a thatched-roofed hut woke up in the morning to find himself in a new metal-roofed house with an orchard around it and Birds of Paradise singing outside. Or maybe one does not have any money, yet prays earnestly and all of a sudden there is a miracle!

If God existed and there were such miracles, people would not fight but live in harmony. All they would have to do is just spend a night in earnest prayer and all would be well.

Do not be offended with me, dear friends. In your programs you always ask us to write, so please read this. And if it is not too much of a bother, send me a reply. I shall be very happy to receive it. In fact, if I were to actually receive a response from you, may it be considered a miracle.

I send you my best wishes and Christmas greetings.

— a listener from Kyrgyzstan

Everywhere Peter Deyneka traveled he found fruit from the "miracle electronic missionary." While speaking at an evangelistic meeting in Argentina one time, Peter was introduced to a young man who had come to sing and play the accordion. Before the man began, he turned to Peter and said, "Mr. Deyneka, you and the people in this meeting don't realize this, but you are my spiritual father. In 1950, I became a Christian through your ministry. I remember well the night when you spoke and I gave my heart to Christ. That night my life was changed.

"In 1957, after I was converted, my parents decided to return to Russia from Argentina. I returned with them, but this was a time of great struggle in my life. I was full of turmoil and sadness. Through much prayer,

I finally realized that being in Russia was God's will for me and I submitted my life to Christ and tried to serve Him there.

"I remember when I arrived with my parents in that Russian village, the people were not acquainted with the Gospel broadcasts from Ecuador. I introduced them to these programs. One man had just sold his radio because he was tired of listening to propaganda. But as soon as he learned about your broadcasts, he bought another radio and started listening to HCJB. 'Why didn't you come to Russia sooner and tell me about these wonderful programs?' he asked. 'Then I could have kept my first radio and wouldn't have had to buy another one. But it was worth it!'

"Shortly after our arrival, many other Christians began listening to the radio broadcasts. I know for a fact that untold thousands of people in the Soviet Union are listening to the Russian-language broadcasts of Slavic Gospel Association. I know, because I lived among those people."

Thus, the long arms of radio embraced the globe. Many will be in heaven because Peter Deyneka followed the Lord's leading and launched a new medium for the Gospel to reach Russians, proving again his obedience to preach the Gospel "by all means" everywhere.

13

ANOTHER FAMINE
OF BREAD

During the 1920s, the Soviet government authorized a major print-ing of Bibles in the Russian language. Again in 1957, 1968, and 1974, they officially sanctioned print runs totaling approximately 50,000 Bibles, specifically for evangelicals. However, those token printings didn't even begin to satisfy the spiritual thirst of Russia's millions.

To counter the widespread hunger for truth, the government stepped up their printing of communist propaganda and a vast proliferation of various atheistic materials. The Soviets would print more books annually than any other country in the world, attempting to divert the attention of the masses. One year they published hundreds of thousands of copies each of 284 different titles devoted to the subject of atheism. In addition, articles on the virtues of atheism were placed in periodicals whose circu-lations ran into the multimillions. By contrast, the output of religious lit-erature that same year was almost zero.

The atheistic government also attempted to create an atmosphere of fear regarding the Bible. The official Soviet encyclopedia stated that the Bible was a compilation of Jewish myths and that Jesus was a mytholog-ical character. "No such person ever existed," the encyclopedia declared. This volume was the official reference used by Russia's 250 million peo-ple, yet the fruitless promises of atheism did not satisfy and many still longed to discover the truth about Jesus Christ. And for those who had come to know the truth and the truth had set them free, their search for the Bread of Life intensified.

When SGA was founded, the demand for Bibles and Gospel literature in Russia had already become desperate. Peter Deyneka was rarely out of earshot of his brethren's pleas for God's Word in print. Thus, he decided "printed missionaries must be part of the SGA program."

Literature has inherent power. It never grows weary, argues, complains, or needs support. It adapts itself to a given culture and speaks even when discarded. Gradually, shelves at SGA headquarters began filling up with a stockpile of Russian-language literature earmarked for Russia and beyond, where it was used in soul-winning expeditions and for Bible-teaching conferences.

On one trip into the desolate region of Siberia, an SGA-sponsored missionary took several Bibles and Christian books. In one large church he gave the pastor a Bible and a copy of *The Life of Jesus Christ*, a picture book of the Gospels for children. The pastor held the pictorial book in his hand, gently and reverently turning the colorful pages with a smile on his face. "This is for children?" he questioned. "Why, even our adults have never seen anything as beautiful as this!"

Other brethren spotted the pastor with the book and began pressing in for a closer look. "We want it next!" they exclaimed.

"You'll have to form a line," the pastor directed, "and sign up on a list so everyone can have a chance."

The line snaked down the aisle and around the outside wall as Christians, eager for devotional materials to read, patiently waited their turn to request a few precious days with the book.

In tears, the pastor thanked the visitor for the gifts. "Two books for 500 people," he sighed. "Could you somehow bring us more?"

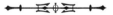

Appeals for Bibles were received at SGA on a continual basis. On each trip overseas, Peter and his co-workers returned with stories of people who were prepared to sacrifice as much as a month's wages to obtain the precious collection of sacred writings.

One Christian man in Russia finally received a Bible after waiting many years. He opened the cover and began to read: "The New Testament of our Lord Jesus Christ." Tears came to his eyes as he said, "This is the most important book in the world. The message of this book will give me new courage."

Another person in the Soviet Union declared, "I am ready to be without anything   but not without the Word of God."

In Ukraine, so many people signed up to have a copy of the Bible for one week that the pastor estimated it would take seven months to serve all who had expressed a wish to take their turn.

One day in Moscow, a Christian brother who had heard Peter speak approached him hesitantly. "Brother Deyneka," he began, "when you are finished with your visit to Russia, what are you going to do with your New Testament?"

"Well, I always carry a New Testament with me . . ."

"But Brother Deyneka, there is a preacher in St. Petersburg who has none. How wonderful it would be if you could give him yours."

When Peter arrived in St. Petersburg to visit the church, he approached the first man he saw inside. "I am looking for Brother Vasily," he said.

"I am he," the Russian replied.

Peter pulled out his New Testament. "Then this is yours as a gift. I apologize that the cover is worn."

The Russian was seized with deep emotion as he eagerly accepted the gift. "Oh, Brother Deyneka, we are not looking for beautiful covers. We are looking for the Word of God!" he exclaimed.

The pastor gently laid the treasure on his desk, then he tenderly lifted it up and looked at it again. He shook Peter's hand enthusiastically in gratitude for the rare and privileged opportunity to personally study God's Word and improve his preaching.

God often used unusual avenues to allow access for Gospel literature to be taken into closed countries by SGA workers and their associates in Western Europe.

Two men — a Russian Christian and an SGA missionary — stood in the bitter, wintry cold one morning in Moscow. The Russian, with a handless arm hanging limply at his side, told the missionary tourist that he had traveled some 5,000 miles with one purpose — to find and take back a Bible so he could "teach God's Word" to his small congregation of believers. The SGA missionary had one Bible left in his hotel room. Seeing the man's faith, he felt compelled to surrender his last Bible to this crippled lay preacher who had traveled so far in search of God's Word.

While the missionary tourist went to his room to get the Bible, the Russian preacher waited in the lobby. When the Bible arrived, the excited preacher embraced the missionary with his good arm and loudly exclaimed in the carefully watched lobby, "God be praised!"

Then, to the consternation of the visitor and to the amazement of the Soviet hotel management, the old minister fearlessly dropped to his knees. Without concern for his own safety he cried, "Let us pray right here! I must thank the Lord immediately for this great gift. I can now return to Siberia — I have found what I came for."

Visiting tourists, like this SGA missionary, were an effective conduit for bringing a great number of Bibles into the communist world at that time. When Christians in the Soviet Union would hear about friends from the West coming to visit them with Christian literature, they would often fast and pray — sometimes as long as a month — for the safe arrival of both the messenger and the message.

Christians also treasured the old Bibles that had been printed many years earlier. The feeble books were bound and rebound, time and again, protected as rare treasures of vintage.

For the majority of Christians, however, their only access to a Bible was to resort to the same methods people used before the printing press was invented — they hand-copied God's Word. Believers would borrow a Bible for a few days in order to copy as much as possible into a notebook, or they would listen to radio broadcasts from overseas and hurriedly attempt to record all the Scripture they heard. Some Christians, over a period of years, managed to copy the entire Bible.

Sometimes when Christians gained possession of a complete Bible, they would divide the book up into sections so that 30 or 40 of their friends could have at least part of the Bible, rather than one person keeping the whole thing for himself. They would then continually circulate the sections. If a borrower kept a portion too long, he would be reminded that others were waiting to use it.

Whenever Peter visited Russia, believers would beg for Bibles, earnestly pleading with him for the Word of God. Many showed him "Bibles" they had copied by hand. Many had to take their turn reading copies lent to them by their pastor.

On one trip, an SGA missionary noticed two women with flimsy top coats in a cold, windy park near a church where he was to speak. One was reading aloud while the other listened. Both ignored the bitter weather.

Quietly a third joined them on the park bench, then a fourth and a fifth. Eventually there were six women huddled on the bench, listening to the reading which was obviously precious. The observer soon realized that the women were Christian believers and their treasure was a copy of God's Word which the owner was sharing in the park.

Visiting a Christian home, that same missionary gave the children of the family a copy of *The Life of Jesus Christ*. The children immediately scampered away with the book and the visitor soon heard them crying. He learned that they all wanted to read the book at the same time. They had never seen a Christian book for youth before.

One of the most grievous experiences for Peter was to meet a Christian who begged for a Bible or some other piece of literature, and then not have it to give to him. He once met a young man after a service in northern Russia, who asked Peter if by any chance he might have a Russian Bible that he could give him. With great regret, Peter told him that he did not — the ones he had brought had already been distributed.

The young Russian told Peter that he lived in Novosibirsk, more than 3,000 miles from the city in which he was now standing. He was spending his entire vacation traveling thousands of miles, at great expense, all for the sole purpose of finding a Bible. The young believer turned away sadly. He had come with such high hopes, only to leave dejectedly, realizing that he might actually return home empty-handed.

During another of his trips to Russia, Peter noticed a man following him as he left the church where he had just preached.

"Brother Deyneka!" the man called. "I plead with you in the name of the Lord, give me your New Testament."

Peter stopped and looked at the stranger sorrowfully. "I'm sorry," he said, "I have no more. I have given them all away."

The man shook his head. "Surely you have *one* more — even your own copy perhaps? I have so longed and hoped for God's Word . . ."

Peter laid a hand on the man's shoulder. "I'm so sorry," he repeated, "I do not have a single copy left."

The man went away grieved, representative of the thousands who so desperately longed to be spiritually nourished by the Bread of Life.

14

MUCH PRAYER — MUCH POWER

Peter Deyneka was never afraid to pray, nor afraid to lose sleep and appeal to God in "strong crying and tears" for the needs of his growing mission. In return, amazing things happened. The heavenly answers were no surprise to Peter — he knew God was listening.

"Little prayer, little power," Peter often admonished his friends, "but much prayer, much power!"

At the start of his Christian life, Peter learned the power of prayer at Cedar Lake Bible Conference in Indiana, founded by Paul Rader in the early 1920s. Paul Rader would announce special men's prayer meetings in the woods near the camp, and he often asked Peter to lead those meetings. Later, in 1930, when Rader was conducting Bible conferences at Lake Harbor, Michigan (now Maranatha Bible Conference), Peter was put in charge of the prayer sessions in a tower overlooking the grounds and Lake Michigan. Peter's enthusiasm for prayer led many to that tower, where lives were transformed and where thousands of dollars were raised for the work of the Lord.

In the early years of the Youth for Christ movement following World War II, Peter's contributions to their efforts were super doses of prayer — all-night sessions which opened the doors of heaven and unleashed spiritual power. Those Deyneka-led prayer meetings became legendary, continuing to occur for 20 consecutive summers.

One YFC rally was scheduled at Chicago's huge Soldier Field on a Memorial Day weekend. For three weeks before the rally it had rained steadily every day, threatening to cancel the event. Much preparation had been made and much money spent on advertising. YFC president Torrey Johnson phoned in an SOS to Peter.

"We must have a 24-hour prayer meeting," Torrey said, "and I want you to lead it, Peter."

Christian leaders, pastors, and laymen gathered at the Sherman Hotel in downtown Chicago to ask God to stop the rain so the meeting could be held. "As we prayed for it to stop, we could hear the rain falling outside," Peter recalls. "It was difficult for some to keep going."

Two hours before the 24-hour prayer vigil was scheduled to end, Peter stopped the meeting. "We have been praying for the rain to stop," he reminded the gathered intercessors. "Let us now spend the final two hours thanking God that there will be no rain tomorrow!"

The next morning, the rain had vanished. Sunshine bathed the rain-soaked city, although for five miles all around Chicago the rain kept falling. More than 65,000 people gathered at Soldier Field to hear the singing, testimonies, and Gospel message. Hundreds of people committed their lives to the Lord Jesus Christ. The service closed and the people went home rejoicing and praising God — and the next day the long siege of rain resumed. It continued to rain for several days afterward.

Through those dynamic YFC prayer meetings during the summers at Winona Lake, Peter became well-acquainted with a young evangelist named Billy Graham whom he had first met while Graham was a student at Trinity Bible College in Florida. In 1949, Graham held his first major citywide crusade in Los Angeles and invited Peter to come spend a few days before the crusade, praying together and seeking God for His blessing on the meetings. Graham was conscious of the fact that without the blessing and power of God upon his ministry, there would be little eternal value accomplished. Their prayers were heard. Many came to Christ.

One summer in Europe, where Peter was speaking on the victorious spiritual life, a woman came to him following one of his messages. "My husband is an unbeliever," she said weeping. "I have lost patience with him."

Peter challenged her: "Stop preaching at him and start praying for him. Live a Christian life in humility before him." Three months later, Peter learned that God had saved her husband in answer to the wife's steady, faithful prayer.

Back in 1922, when Peter had received that dreadful letter informing him that his family was dying from starvation, he spent a day and night in prayer for his parents and brother, Andrei, who had not yet perished. His appetite left him. In desperation, he would not give up praying until he felt assured that God would answer and help his family.

The morning after his all-night prayer vigil, a Christian friend came to see him. "I have not been able to sleep because of a burden," she admitted. "Do you have someone in Russia to whom you could send money?"

Peter asked how she knew about the terrible suffering his parents were going through.

"God laid it on my heart and I felt there must be a need," she replied. And that was the source of the funds God provided for Peter to send overseas so his family could buy food.

During his first visit to his parents' home before his mother accepted Christ, Peter was met with intense opposition. The more he prayed for his mother, the more disturbed she became. "This showed that the Holy Spirit was working in her heart," said a determined Peter, "so I kept praying — more than ever."

When Peter returned to the United States without seeing his mother take the step of faith, he continued praying, undeterred — even when letters from home remained cold and indifferent. "My hope was in Christ," Peter said. He endured estrangement for nearly a year, but "the effective, fervent prayer of a righteous man avails much" (James 5:16) and Peter's mother eventually accepted the saving grace of Jesus Christ.

His brother Andrei, a confirmed unbeliever, also came under conviction through prayer. "The more you pray for me, the worse I feel and the more I suffer," he told Peter. So Peter prayed harder, and God broke a proud, stubborn heart and brought a committed atheist to Himself.

Whether raising his children, guiding SGA through troubled waters, preparing to preach, or conducting one-on-one evangelism, prayer was Peter's divine weapon in life. He once prayed diligently for a fellow Russian in Chicago because the young man leaned toward atheism. The Russian merely laughed at him, but Peter promised: "I will not stop praying for you until God saves your soul."

"Well, you'll be praying for a long time then," the young man replied.

"If you die without God, you'll find out too late that He does indeed exist," Peter warned, continuing to faithfully pray for the man for more than a year, even enlisting the prayer support of others.

One afternoon, a friend of Peter's also agreed to pray for a full two hours on behalf of the unsaved Slavic man. The following morning, Peter went to the store where the atheist worked. As he approached the man's department, the Russian looked up with surprise.

"Peter!" he exclaimed. "I'm so glad you came to see me. Yesterday I had no rest and I thought I would die. I didn't know what to do with myself. I felt miserable." He told Peter of the terrible suffering his heart had endured.

"Praise the Lord," Peter said. "We were praying for you last night."

"Please don't pray anymore," the friend pleaded. "I'll do whatever you tell me to do."

"You must give your heart to the Lord at once," Peter explained.

The man promised to be at Moody Memorial Church on Sunday at 3:00 p.m. for the young men's Bible class, and he was there. When the teacher gave the invitation for salvation, the young fellow walked forward. He knelt at the altar and wept, giving his heart to the Lord. With his life straightened out, he married a Christian girl and entered into the blessing of a Christ-centered marriage.

Such incidents were common in the life of Peter Deyneka. He allowed God to lead him to people with hungry hearts, and God kept him busy on fruitful assignments.

Peter's wife was his most faithful and enduring prayer partner. Vera learned to pray at the start of her Christian life, even before she met Peter during his preaching mission to Russia. She began her Christian life under great oppression from an unsaved family and had to lean heavily on the Lord to fortify her against misunderstanding parents, brothers, and sisters. Her lonely spiritual crusade taught her early on to pray diligently.

Missionary Hubert Mitchell of Los Angeles felt a kinship with Peter Deyneka as he participated in the meetings at the old Billy Sunday Tabernacle and in the hillside services at Winona Lake.

"Peter would literally lay hold of the altar in nights of prayer," Mitchell recalled. "When everyone else was falling by the wayside, Peter was constantly hounding heaven for the sake of evangelism — especially for the Russian nation. I believe those nights of prayer deposited some holy seeds that have sprouted many times and brought forth the harvest, not only here but in other countries as well."

During YFC evangelistic conferences in Ireland, Belgium, Venezuela, and Brazil, Peter Deyneka headed the prayer groups. Robert A. Cook, an early YFC president who later became president of King's College, labeled Peter's ministry "a power quite beyond the natural gifts with which

God had endowed him." Whenever Peter was in Bob Cook's area, not many days would go by before he would stop by his office and say, "Well brother, let's pray!"

Peter believed that unless prayer became frontal, deliberate, and planned — rather than a luxury or an accessory — the Christian could expect little of a miraculous nature. Bob Cook grasped that fact early in his leadership. He passed the word throughout Youth for Christ that if young men wanted to remain in top administrative positions within the organization, the price of that leadership would be prayer.

Peter Deyneka's method for extended periods of prayer would begin with a time of prayer, then a time of praise, then Bible teaching, then testimonies from people in whose life God had been working. At the close of the second session of prayer, the leader would provide an invitation.

Bob Cook observed, "I learned that people make their best speeches to God in the early hours of those extended prayer meetings. But later on, they get around to telling God the real truth about the situation. And sometimes the Holy Spirit of God breaks through to heart and mind and conscience in a way that makes the individual willing to deal with matters in ways he may have been quite inflexible to face just two or three hours earlier. I remember one young man who boldly prayed a very articulate prayer along about 11:00, yet by 1:30 in the morning an invitation was given and this same young man said softly with his head bowed, 'Will somebody please pray for me? I am not saved.'"

＊—＋ ⊫◊⊐ ＋—＊

Some amusing incidents linger in the minds of those who participated in prayer meetings led by Peter Deyneka. With Peter, there was no toying with any subject — prayer requests were confidently pronounced and God was implored for answers. His energy and fervor would frequently raise the volume of his voice a few decibels above normal.

One evening Peter was directing an all-night prayer meeting at the old Westminster Hotel in Winona Lake, Indiana. At about 2:00 a.m., he began to warm up to his usual "level" and his prayers began to rise to the floors above the main conference room where they were meeting. Soon, there was a knock on the door. It was the clerk at the front desk asking, "Could Mr. Deyneka please lower his voice so guests upstairs could get some sleep?"

One of the men took the message to Peter and tapped him on the shoulder. "You know, Peter, God isn't deaf."

"No," Peter replied, "and He isn't nervous either!" He went right on praying without missing a beat.

In another prayer meeting, while praying for a number of people, Peter became confused with the names and got them all mixed up. He paused for a moment to try and collect his thoughts, then finally said, "Sorry, Lord — wrong number."

In Charleston, West Virginia, Peter arrived in town for meetings just ahead of the worst blizzard that part of the country had seen in a long time. He and the men who had gathered with him were literally marooned in their hotel by the storm. Yes, Peter initiated a prayer meeting.

"Lord, why did you do this to me?" he wondered aloud. "You know that I set aside this time to come here for a meeting. You also know that I am busy and could hardly spare the time. Now why would You send a blizzard to stop the meeting? Yet You knew all this, so I'm just going to trust You for what You want to do."

A handful of people did manage to make it through the howling storm to the meeting that night, and one of them gave a large check for the work of SGA. As always, God knew what He was doing.

One day while distributing tracts in Minneapolis, Peter walked up to a man who was dressed in overalls and appeared despondent.

"Pardon me, may I help you?" Peter asked.

The man looked at him in surprise. "How do you know I need help?" he asked.

"I prayed and asked God to lead me to someone who needed help," Peter explained.

"I have a wife and two children," the man began, "and here I am out on the street. I was so drunk my wife asked me to leave. I am broken-hearted — not so much for my wife, but I love my two precious children. Now I have no home and there's no hope that things will get better . . ."

"There is hope in Christ," Peter assured him.

They went to a nearby Gospel rescue mission where the lonely man knelt down. "I need God's help. Please pray for me."

Peter received a letter one week later. The man's home was 200 miles from Minneapolis, but he had found a way home, had asked forgiveness of his family, and had been completely restored to them. Prayer had led Peter to a man who needed God.

"It pays to pray that God will lead and guide you," Peter always said with characteristic simplicity. "The Bible says in James 1:5, 'If any of you lacks wisdom, let him ask of God, who gives to all liberally . . .'"

The Lord also heard Peter and Vera's prayers regarding their children. "My wife and I have had the joy of leading all three of them to the Lord Jesus Christ. I also had the joy of baptizing each of them. All three have received training at Christian colleges and have dedicated their lives to the Lord's service.

"Because God answers prayer, He has opened doors for us to work and to preach the Gospel in more than 22 countries around the world, with more than 140 missionaries preaching in 20 languages. Scores and scores of souls are being won for the Lord. Thousands are hearing the Gospel who otherwise would never have heard, and much clothing and food have been sent to poor Christians in Europe."

Peter Deyneka was a living example of his motto, "Much prayer — much power." His recipe was simple: "When you go to pray, pour out your heart before God. Claim His promises. Claim the victory. Ask God to cleanse your heart, mind, and even your thoughts. When David prayed in Psalm 139:23 he said, 'Search me, O God, and know my heart; try me, and know my thoughts.' He not only asked God to search his heart, but also to search his thoughts.

"If we meet God's conditions when we come to pray, He has promised to do His part. Our part is to come to Him, to seek Him, ask of Him, in faith and sincerity with a pure heart, in His name and authority, and He will hear and answer our prayers.

"Do you love the Lord? Then take time to talk to Him. A prayer of faith will accomplish great things."

15

THE CRY FROM THE STEPPES

At SGA's Chicago headquarters one morning, Peter Deyneka opened an unusual letter from Russia with postmarks indicating the sender lived in the town of Peter's birth:

> In the morning of May 13, 1974, I heard you preaching here in Russia from Radio Station HCJB. At first I did not recognize your voice, but later when you gave your name I remembered you. For a long time now I have wanted to hear your voice, but never had the opportunity. The broadcast signal that morning was very clear and without any interference. Every word was clear.

Peter wept as he continued to read:

> I still remember your visit to our country 40 years ago. From our town you went to the city of Chomsk. There was a big meeting there, during which many people were baptized. My sister and I attended this meeting and we had to walk 50 kilometers [30 miles] in order to get there. It took us an entire day. We weren't tired because when we got there we experienced such great blessing. I will never forget it.
>
> All of this came back to me as I was listening to your voice over the radio. I'm so thankful I met you at that par-

ticular baptismal service. With all of my heart, I am grateful to
God for these broadcasts and for the joy of hearing your voice
again. May the Lord bless you and keep you in His work.

As Peter laid the letter on his desk, the years of memories rolled back
to that first broadcast in 1941 when he stopped at radio station HCJB en
route home from his first trip to Argentina. His close friend, Clarence
Jones, had offhandedly remarked, "Why don't you try preaching over the
radio in Russian, Peter? Let's see if any Russians somewhere in the world
are listening."

So many Russians in the Soviet Union tuned in to the Gospel broadcasts that Soviet newspapers discouraged their citizens from listening. The
authorities publicly complained about Russian-language programs from
foreign radio stations sweeping across the country "like ocean waves."
Reports from inside the Soviet Union indicated that millions of Russian
citizens had their shortwave radios set to receive Christian programs.

Peter Deyneka met many of them during his travels throughout Russia. He only needed to say his name to have an entire congregation brighten
with recognition: "You are the Pyotr who speaks on the radio broadcasts!"

Believers all across Russia would inform Peter: "We fast and pray on
the first Friday of every month, asking God to continue to bless and encourage the Church in the West to help us save millions of our people
through your broadcasts."

In one church, a babushka (elderly grandmother) told Peter with a
smile, "The broadcasts drop out of the air like a gift from heaven to us."

Russian Christians were always eager to share with Peter stories about
how the broadcasts brought their countrymen to Christ. One man in the
remote region of Siberia had never seen a Bible, never attended church,
and never met another Christian. But he came to saving faith in Jesus
Christ through a message he heard from a radio preacher.

In another town, a man found the courage to preach by listening to
the radio broadcasts. He wanted to attend a seminary, but of course there
were none at the time, so he listened to SGA's *Bible Institute of the Air*
and other programs and received a sound theological education.

"Whole villages have come to Christ through the broadcasts," Slavic
Christians told Peter. He saw for himself how the broadcasts had become
Bible, preacher, and Sunday school for multiplied thousands deprived of
these spiritual blessings.

It is impossible to know how many letters sent by listeners never got past Soviet censors. But thousands each year did make it through, many of which contained interesting stories and comments . . .

Peace to you, dear brother and all your co-workers. All of us listen to you with great joy — not just believers, but also unbelievers have a great desire to listen to your programs. At times one walks along the street and hears the broadcast from Monte Carlo coming from apartments, in spite of the fact that many must listen at a low volume so that no one will discover that they do listen.

There are those who have come to repentance listening to the radio in their homes. One backslider, having heard your message, repented and once again follows the Lord. In one village, an unbeliever bought himself a radio receiver. His neighbors came to hear it, and as he was turning the dial they heard wonderful singing. They realized it was something religious and started to listen. They heard the message and were deeply under conviction, looking with bewilderment at the radio. "How is it that he, being so far away, speaks as if he sees us?" they began questioning among themselves. "Listen! He is talking about us!" And they broke down weeping.

That is the way the preaching of the Gospel affects the hearers, "for it is the power of God to salvation for everyone who believes" (Romans 1:16). Praise be unto the Lord.

— from a listener in Poland

Hello, dear friends. For two years I have been listening to your broadcasts, but haven't been able to write because I was serving in the army. I want to pass on some good news.

Thanks to the religious broadcasts, I have become a believer and have received Jesus Christ into my heart. The work which you are doing is great and indispensable. I, for one, wish to thank you for broadcasting the Word of God to my homeland. I am 22 years old, single, and have secondary education. I continue to listen to your broadcasts and would like you to help me get a Bible and Gospel literature.

— a Russian soldier

First of all, I want to convey to you heartfelt greetings in the name of our Lord. On a recent journey I visited many churches and had numerous meetings with brothers and sisters. I am very thankful to the Lord for these opportunities. What I experienced I can never forget. In one village, the small church had been isolated for a long time, but one Gospel program finally managed to get through and a great many people were saved. Many churches pray for you, but we have to be careful. I anxiously await your answer.

— a letter from Belarus

So wrote members of the Slavic brotherhood of believers. Amidst their immense struggles and hardships, conversions were common. Regardless of what the Soviet authorities would have had people believe, the church in Russia was not dying — it was alive and well.

Despite its impact on Soviet society, the Russian church at the time lacked visible organization. It appeared almost primitive by the standards of a sophisticated Western church structure. However, the Russian church in all of its adversity and simplicity offered insights to Western Christians. The West had a proliferation of church organizations, seminaries, youth groups, publishing houses, and Bibles — while the Russians had *none* of those spiritual luxuries — yet they were still an example for all.

During Soviet times, the Russian church was predominantly a lay church. There were few full-time pastors and each congregation traditionally had from 20 to 40 lay preachers. That way, there were many prepared to lead the church. If one was taken or removed by authorities, another could quickly step into his place.

But it was also a lay church because of the lack of Bible schools and seminaries to produce bona fide clergy. With no opportunities for formal Bible training, Russian believers depended heavily on Gospel radio broadcasts. Peter Deyneka met thousands of people who repeatedly thanked him for the programs. One pastor said apologetically, "I hope you don't mind, brother. I copy down the sermon outlines from your broadcasts so I can preach them to my people. I have no other study materials."

Although there were numerous things the Russian church could not do, they could pray. One pastor put it this way; "As Christians facing pressures and problems, we can't effectively protest, but we can pray. We can pray until the building shakes, as the early persecuted Christian church did in the Acts of the Apostles." This spiritual discipline of prayer established a powerful tradition that continues to this day.

Russian believers are known for how they pray. They are true prayer warriors — and therein lies great spiritual power. Pastors pray several times in each service. Others join in total supplication. From all across the sanctuary, one may hear muffled cries of "Da Gospodee [Yes, Lord]," in response to the prayers. When members are given an opportunity to pray aloud, there is no hesitation. Prayers from believers with compelling burdens rise in intercession. Often, so many wish to participate that the pastor is forced to interrupt and close the prayer session.

The passion for prayer is probably responsible for also laying the foundation for hearts of evangelism. Pastors and church leaders are typically quite curious about Christian activity and missionary endeavors occurring in the West. Russian believers feel deeply responsible for missionary outreach. As one believer said thoughtfully, "Here in Russia, every Christian is a missionary."

Yet Russian believers aren't spiritual supermen. They are ordinary people who frequently become discouraged by their unstable society, yet they do not ask to be removed from their country. They still plead for Western churches to not forget them. They still need our help.

✦ ✦ ✦

These are the people of Peter Deyneka. For more than half a century he represented them to the world — speaking out for those who could not leave, evangelizing many who settled in other lands, placing in their hands the tools for Gospel witnessing, and serving as a channel from generous brothers and sisters in free countries wishing to support them. There was no stopping him. And from that one man with a vision, SGA has become an international organization touching millions of lives with the Gospel of Jesus Christ.

On one autumn day during one of his last visits to the Soviet Union, Peter Deyneka found himself with a small congregation of believers deep in the heart of Russia. That morning six new converts, robed in white, stood at the front of the church near the baptistry. Each of the six Christians understood the cost of his commitment to follow Christ in baptism. Those who had been followers of Christ longer had carefully prepared the converts for the momentous step of baptism — a Christian ceremony particularly despised by atheist authorities. Many of the believers in the congregation held flowers which would later be presented to the person who was prepared to obey Christ by entering the waters of baptism.

The pastor, a humble man in a dark suit and white beard, waited on each candidate as the other Christians sang hymns of praise. As one of the women was helped from the baptistry, the people gathered around and offered their flowers which she accepted gratefully. When her bouquet was received, she turned to the visiting evangelist and extended it.

"Brother Deyneka," she said, "you must have these. If it had not been for your radio broadcasts, I would not be a Christian today."

Peter took the flowers and looked at them, the petals gently quivering in his trembling hand. Although presented to him, he knew that they were given in thanksgiving for what God had done.

"Thank you, Father," he prayed. "You have answered my prayers. You have not left my people without a witness."

"Da Gospodee [Yes, Lord]," the people murmured in response.

*Peter's humble,
thatched-roof home
in the village of
Staramlynia.*

*The first photograph
of Peter, a determined
15-year-old, upon his
arrival in Chicago
— a photo which he
promptly sent back
to his parents
in Russia.*

*A joyful Peter
with the smile that
"wouldn't go away"
after his conversion
on January 18, 1920.*

*Peter loved evangelism
and joined several
summer outreach
teams during
his student days.*

When Peter first returned to Russia in 1925, his surviving mother and brother were overjoyed to see him — but not so quick to embrace his newfound faith.

New converts near Peter's birthplace, marching to the river for baptism during the great spiritual awakening that occurred during his first trip home.

In those early days of pioneer evangelism, Peter often traveled by horse, including the wild stallion that had some wondering if eager Peter was a "Russian Cossack."

Peter married Vera Demidovich, a quiet Russian girl, on May 23, 1926.

The first faculty and student body of the Russian Bible Institute in Toronto — the school built on prayer.

The Peter Deyneka family, circa 1944 — (left to right) Ruth, Peter Jr., Lydia, Vera, and Peter.

No matter how many Bibles and Christian books were printed, it didn't begin to quench the spiritual thirst for truth.

The Russian staff at HCJB Radio — (left to right) Const and Elizabeth Lewshenia, Stella Jarema, Helen Zernov, Vera Deyneka, Ruth and Jack Shalanko, and Peter (seated).

Peter's explosive preaching style, coupled with his zealous desire to win the lost, was the source of his nickname Peter Dynamite.

Peter living his dream — preaching to his beloved countrymen in his beloved country.

Large crowds of believers gather around Peter after a morning service to express gratitude for the "bread of heaven" they receive over the airwaves.

One of the last photos of Peter, taken at SGA's 50th anniversary just a few years before his death.

EPILOGUE
BY RUTH DEYNEKA ERDEL

When I look back on my life, my heart is full of praise to God for my wonderful Russian family. Growing up in Chicago, my brother (Peter Jr.), sister (Lydia), and I had a childhood full of love and joy. We laughed a lot! Yet the entire atmosphere in our home was guided by caring parents who steeped everything in prayer. Their only purpose and desire in life was to take the Gospel to Russian-speaking people, so our daily routine was entirely geared toward that vision.

During the many times my father was away from home, preaching overseas or conducting services in the United States or Canada, we would beg our mother to tell us stories about their childhood in Russia. After our nightly time of prayer together, we would huddle under the covers and ask her questions: "What did Papa's house look like? Was the water in the well very cold? Was there a fence around the house? Did you really climb the cherry tree in front of your house?" Lying in bed, I drew many pictures in my mind of my father's childhood home in the small village of Staramlynia.

In 1993, I stood at the end of a dirt road and looked back at that same house for the very first time. I saw the well alongside it and the surrounding fence, now broken down in many places because of age. I kicked the dirt and imagined my father playing with his brothers and sisters in that dust while growing up in such immense poverty. It was no longer an imaginary picture in my mind. I was actually standing on the road looking at the home itself.

It was from this spot that my father left his home on March 3, 1914, a lad of only 15 years of age, to travel to America. His father was anticipating that the money he would send back home would help his family survive their dire financial situation. My father accepted this responsibility and started his journey to a new world.

In Chicago, he did find a job and eventually helped his family out of debt, but he was lonely. One Sunday while out walking, he heard Russians singing. The singers were Christians who took interest in this lonely lad and encouraged him to attend Moody Memorial Church. Under the ministry of Dr. Paul Rader, on January 18, 1920, he accepted the Lord into his heart.

Many times as a young girl, I heard my father quote Psalm 142:4. With tears he would say, "I looked, but there was no man who would help me. No man cared for my soul." With this challenge that grew out of his own lonely young life, my father had but one vision. With all his heart, his desire was to take the Gospel message to Russian-speaking people around the world.

In 1934, when my father founded SGA, the office took up the area of our second bedroom. We children had to sleep in the dining room on a day bed, but we thought it was the greatest fun. When there were special financial needs for the mission, we were encouraged to join our parents in prayer — on our knees — asking the Lord for His help and guidance. I think this is one reason why we never expected to have extra things that were not important. We were taught to see the needs of others.

One day in conversation with my mother, I expressed sadness that Papa was always gone and we never went on fancy vacations like our school friends. I remember how quickly my mother called Lydia, Peter Jr. and me together and pulled all three of us to our knees. "Dietki [children]," she said, "how privileged we are that God has called Papa to preach the Gospel. Right now he is in a church meeting. Let's pray together that someone will ask Jesus to come into his heart tonight." With that, my dear mother's voice rang out in such wonderful prayer of thanksgiving to the Lord. From that moment on, I never complained again. I learned the joy my parents had in serving Christ, and this is what influenced our lives as children to always want to live for Him and serve Him.

From my earliest years, I have precious memories of our family always going to church together. Many times my mother would sing a solo, and then my father would call on my brother and me to sing and to quote a Bible verse in both Russian and English before his sermon. Our parents encouraged us to be friendly with people and to talk with them after the services. Missionaries and pastors frequently stayed in our home, and we enjoyed their stories.

"Much prayer, much power," were not just words my father said in the pulpit. My father lived this statement. My parents did everything with prayer. Yes, people called him Peter Dynamite because he was indeed like dynamite — powerfully explosive about getting the Gospel of Jesus Christ out to all the world.

Over 70 years have passed since my father founded SGA in 1934, and those 70 years have been consumed by continuing his vision of reaching out to Slavic people around the world — sending out missionaries, planting churches, supporting pastors and church planters and supplying them with ministry tools, printing Bibles and Christian literature, starting and supporting Bible-teaching institutions, producing videos and radio programs, assisting with church construction, developing programs to nurture orphans and other children, assisting with humanitarian aid . . . the list goes on and on.

Standing on that dirt road outside my father's childhood home, I could not stop the tears that flowed down my cheeks. How wonderfully God had rescued young Peter, brought him to America, called him to Himself, then used his life to bring salvation to many souls. From my earliest recollections until the day he died on July 26, 1987, he was a loving father who lived his life completely dedicated to taking God's Word to his Russian-speaking people. His godly example graphically displayed that much prayer really does bring much power — and much joy! What a great privilege God gave me to be his daughter.

SLAVIC GOSPEL ASSOCIATION

SGA is a global, nondenominational, evangelical mission organization founded in 1934 by Peter Deyneka Sr., a Russian immigrant with a deep concern for the spiritual well-being of his compatriots wherever they were to be found. After the fall of the Iron Curtain, profound political and economic changes spread across the former Soviet Union and Central and Eastern Europe. Today, SGA's ministries are concentrated in these regions with the aim of serving the local, indigenous, evangelical churches to bring the Gospel of Jesus Christ to their own peoples. Through a unified strategy, SGA ministries in Australia, Canada, France, New Zealand, the United Kingdom, and the United States work together to that end.

SGA carries out a multifaceted range of missionary outreach including media ministries (Bibles, literature, radio, and TV) based increasingly within the target countries themselves, training of nationals for pastoral ministries and church planting, sponsorship of church planters, pastor training conferences, music and youth ministries, children's work, prison ministries, church construction assistance, and the provision of humanitarian aid for distribution by the local churches. Regional ministry centers are maintained in Moscow and Omsk (Russia), Minsk (Belarus), and Kiev (Ukraine) to support the ministry and outreach of national churches in the former Soviet Union.

In 1997, SGA accepted the invitation of the Russian Union of Evangelical Christians-Baptists (UECB) to become their official representative in the United States, Australia, Canada and New Zealand. Training, equipping, and supporting ministries are assisting Bible-preaching churches in Russia, Ukraine, Belarus, Moldova, Armenia, Kazakhstan, Uzbekistan, Tajikistan, Turkmenistan, Azerbaijan, Abkhazia, Albania, Poland, the Czech and Slovak Republics, Hungary, Romania, Bulgaria, Macedonia, Croatia, and Serbia.

If you would like to learn more about SGA and its many ministries, please contact:

Australia
Slavic Gospel Association
P.O. Box 396, Noble Park, Victoria 3174
sgaaust@starnet.com.au ~ www.sga.org.au

Canada
Slavic Gospel Association
55 Fleming Drive #26, Cambridge, Ontario N1T 2A9
canada@sga.org

France
Association Evangelique Slave
Rue de Mauberge, 59164 Marpent
bill.kapitaniuk@wanadoo.fr

New Zealand
Slavic Gospel Association
P.O. Box 10-156, 591 Dominion Road, Balmoral, Auckland 1004
sganz@clear.net.nz

United Kingdom
Slavic Gospel Association
37A The Goffs, Eastbourne, East Sussex BN21 1HF
office@sga.org.uk ~ www.sga.org.uk

United States
Slavic Gospel Association
6151 Commonwealth Drive, Loves Park, Illinois 61111
info@sga.org ~ www.sga.org